On Extraction from Subjects:
An Excorporation Account

On Extraction from Subjects:
An Excorporation Account

Hiroki Egashira

KAITAKUSHA

Kaitakusha Co., Ltd.
5-2, Mukogaoka 1-chome
Bunkyo-ku, Tokyo 113-0023
Japan

On Extraction from Subjects: An Excorporation Account

Published in Japan
by Kaitakusha Co., Ltd., Tokyo

Copyright © 2016
by Hiroki Egashira

All rights reserved. No part of this publication may be reproduced, stored in a retrieval system, or transmitted, in any form or by any means, electronic, mechanical, photocopying, recording, or otherwise, without the prior permission of the copyright owner.

First published 2016

Printed and bound in Japan
by ARM Corporation

Cover design by Shihoko Nakamura

Preface

This book is concerned with the extraction of interrogative *wh*-phrases out of subjects. The extraction of a *wh*-phrase out of a subject is strictly prohibited, as captured by the Subject Condition of Chomsky (1973), which prohibits extraction of a *wh*-phrase out of a subject. This condition is just a description, not an explanation, however; and while the many explanations that have been proposed have become more ingenious as the frameworks have become more elaborate, there seem to me to remain some phenomena that they cannot deal with.

This book has three main aims. One is to reanalyze the Subject Condition within the framework of Minimalism and provide a more comprehensive theory encompassing cases that the previous analyses cannot deal with. Another aim is to extend our analysis of the subextraction of a *wh*-phrase out of a subject to total extraction of a *wh*-subject, showing that the proposed analysis for subextraction can also account for total extraction without ancillary assumptions. The third aim is to provide a unified theory of total extraction and subextraction of a *wh*-phrase both from a subject and from an object.

This book is organized as follows. Chapter 1 presents the goals of this study and introduces a set of basic concepts minimally necessary to understand the discussion in the following chapters. Chapter 2 points out some problems with Chomsky's latest analysis and proposes an alternative analysis, with the aid of a crucial tool for structure building, namely, Excorporation Analysis by Tonoike (2008a, b). Chapter 3 analyzes the total extraction of a *wh*-phrase out of a subject—more specifically, the Complementizer-Copy effect (traditionally known as the *that-/for*-trace effect). Chapter 4 extends the analysis of total and subextraction of a *wh*-subject to that of a *wh*-object, showing that the same conditions that allow extraction of a *wh*-subject always hold in extraction of a *wh*-phrase from an object of a verb and a preposition. Chapter 5 shows how our analysis derives subextracted and totally extracted *wh*-subjects from passive and unaccusative subjects. Chapter 6 summarizes the argument and presents conclusions of this study.

This book is a slightly revised version of my doctoral dissertation submitted to Aoyama Gakuin University in December 2014.

I would like to express my deepest gratitude to Shigeo Tonoike, chair of my doctoral thesis committee, for his generous and invaluable comments and advice. Without his warmhearted assistance and guidance over the years, I could not have finished the dissertation. It was with him that I first experienced the excitement of generative grammar in his undergraduate classes at Meiji Gakuin University.

I also wish to thank the other members of my doctoral committee, especially Kazuo Nakazawa and Heizo Nakajima, who offered me extensive comments and suggestions. Shin'ichi Takeuchi also served as a valued committee member.

Heizo Nakajima used to be my supervisor in the graduate school at Tokyo Metropolitan University. I appreciate his willingness to serve as an outside member of the committee. Without his previous instruction at the Tokyo Metropolitan University graduate school, I could not have completed my dissertation.

I am grateful to Ken-ichi Takami and Kazuyoshi Yamanouchi, who attended the ALL (Aoyama Linguistic and Literature) meeting where I presented the core idea of my dissertation. They gave me useful comments and remarks.

My thanks also go to my young friend Yohei Takahashi, who helped me edit my dissertation at the final stage. I am very glad that he was also able to submit his own dissertation a year later and receive his Ph.D. degree from Aoyama Gakuin University.

In addition, I am thankful to my long-time friend Isamu Gyoda, who is a professional colleague of mine in the Department of Comparative Culture at Otsuma Women's University. He helped me with my work in the department and gave me time to concentrate on my studies. His way of thinking about theoretical matters, from the standpoint of Functional Grammar, stimulated and challenged my way of thinking from that of Generative Grammar.

I also thank all the members of the study group that meets at Aoyama Gakuin University on Friday evenings.

My deepest thanks go to my mother, Fumiyo Egashira. She made it possible for me to get higher education by running a small Chinese restaurant, "Jyogenro."

The publication of this book is supported in part by JSPS KAKENHI Grant Number JP16HP5070.

Contents

Preface ··· v

Chapter 1 Goals and Framework ·· 1
  1.1. Goals ·· 1
  1.2. General Framework ··· 4
    1.2.1. The Model of Grammar ··· 5
    1.2.2. Features ·· 6
    1.2.3. Agree ·· 8
    1.2.4. Merge ··· 9
    1.2.5. Bare Phrase Structure ·· 11
    1.2.6. Derivation ··· 12

Chapter 2 On the Subject Condition ··· 21
  2.1. Phase-Based Approach to the Subject Condition ································ 21
  2.2. Some Problems ·· 29
  2.3. An Alternative Analysis ··· 32
    2.3.1. Theoretical Assumptions: The Excorporation Analysis
         and the Inactivity Condition ··· 32
    2.3.2. An Excorporation Solution ··· 41
    2.3.3. Subextraction from Matrix Clause Subjects ······························· 57

Chapter 3 Total Extraction 71
3.1. Pre-Minimalist Approach 72
  3.1.1. Chomsky's (1986a) Approach: Rigid Minimality 72
  3.1.2. Rizzi's (1990) Approach: Relativized Minimality 74
  3.1.3. Problems with Pre-Minimalist Analyses 78
3.2. The Excorporation Analysis 81
  3.2.1. *For*-Copy Effects 82
  3.2.2. *That*-Copy Effects 86
  3.2.3. Extraction from an Infinitival Subject of the Complement Clause of *want* 95
3.3. Rizzi and Shlonsky (2007) 103
  3.3.1. The Subject Criterion 103
  3.3.2. The Subject Criterion and Overt Complementizer-Copy Effects 110
  3.3.3. Some Problems and Their Solutions 112

Chapter 4 Extraction from Objects 117
4.1. Extraction from Objects and Its Problems 117
4.2. A Solution 123
  4.2.1. Simultaneous Syntactic Relation and the RIC 124
  4.2.2. The Nature of the Simultaneous Syntactic Relation 128
4.3. Extraction from Subjects of ECM 132
4.4. Extraction from Subjects of Other Types of Object-Raising Constructions 140
  4.4.1. Extraction from a Subject of an Acc-*ing* Gerund 140
  4.4.2. Extraction from a Subject of a Perceptual or Causative Construction 150

Chapter 5 Extraction from Subjects of Passive and Unaccusative Predicates 155
5.1. Extraction from Subjects of Passive Predicates 155
5.2. Extraction from Subjects of Unaccusative Predicates 165
5.3. Extraction from the Unaccusative Predicate *arrive* 179
5.4. Agreement in *there*-Constructions 185
5.5. Summary 187

Chapter 6 Summary and Conclusion **189**

References **195**

Index **201**

Chapter 1

Goals and Framework

1.1. Goals

Since the advent of Generative Grammar, one of the main topics of investigation has been how to give a principled explanation to subject-object asymmetries. One type of subject-object asymmetry can be observed in *wh*-extraction, as exemplified in (1).

(1) a. What did you find?
    b. Of which driver did you find a picture?
    c. Who caused an accident?[1]
    d. *Of which car did the driver cause an accident?

The sentences in (1) are *wh*-interrogative sentences. *Wh*-extraction occurs from an object position in (a) and (b) and from a subject position in (c) and (d). In (1a) and (1c) the object and the subject are extracted by the *wh*-movement operation; in (1b) and (1d), on the other hand, a part of the subject and a part of the object are extracted by the *wh*-movement operation. In this book we will call the former type of *wh*-extraction "total extraction" and the latter type "subextraction." As shown in (1d), subextraction of a *wh*-phrase from a subject gives rise to ungrammaticality. This is known as the Subject Condition and the constituent occupying the subject

---

[1] Although change of the word order is not observed in (1c), we assume that the subject *wh*-phrase undergoes *wh*-movement to sentence-initial position, where it takes scope over the sentence.

position that risists wh-extraction is known as Subject Island.

Another type of subject-object asymmetry can be observed in *wh*-extraction from an embedded clause, as shown in (2).

(2) a. Who do you think that Mary will see?
  b. Who do you think Mary will see?
  c. *Who do you think that will see Mary?
  d. Who do you think will see Mary?

In (2a) and (2b), *wh*-extraction takes place from the object position and the *wh*-phrase moves across an embedded declarative clause. The grammaticality of these sentences is not degraded, whether or not the embedded clause is headed by an overt complementizer *that*. In (2c) and (2d), on the other hand, *wh*-extraction takes place from the subject position of the embedded clause, and the grammaticality is degraded when the embedded clause is headed by an overt complementizer *that*. This phenomenon described in (2c) is known as the "*that*-trace effect."

Focusing on the first case of subject-object asymmetry observed in (1), let us first briefly review how Generative Grammar has heretofore analyzed Subject Condition observed in (1d). The sentence in (1d) is considered to have the following derivation.

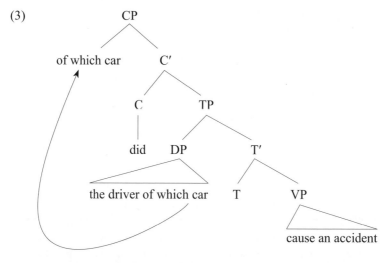

(3)

In (3), the *wh*-phrase is subextracted from the subject position and grammaticality is degraded as a result. In order to capture the fact that nothing can be extracted out of a subject, Chomsky (1973) proposed a Subject Condition, as in (4) below.

(4) Subject Condition
No rule can involve X, Y in the structure $...X...[_\alpha...Y...]...$ where α is a subject phrase properly containing the minimal major category containing Y, and Y is subjacent to X.

In (3) X is the *wh*-phrase in Spec-C, Y is the original position of the *wh*-phrase, and α is the subject *the driver of which car*. The notion "Y is subjacent to X" in the definition of (4) means that there is a cyclic node, which is either NP (= DP) or S′ (= CP), between X and Y. In (3) there is a subject DP between X and Y, and thus, (4) correctly rules out (3).

Taking into consideration the asymmetry between *wh*-extraction from subjects and that from objects (of transitive verbs), Huang (1982) proposed Condition on Extraction Domain (henceforth, CED).

(5) Condition on Extraction Domain
A phrase A may be extracted out of a Domain B only if B is properly governed.

The *wh*-phrase *of which car* in (a) and (b) of (1) can be (sub-)extracted because the complement of the verb is always properly governed by the verb *find*, whereas that in (1d) cannot be extracted because the subject position is not properly governed: The Complementizer *(did)* that c-commands the subject is not a proper governor by definition, while T (or Infl) does not c-command the subject.

Chomsky (1981, 1986a) made an attempt to subsume Huang's CED under the Subjacency Condition and the Empty Category Principle (ECP) in the framework of Government and Binding (GB) Theory. The subject phrase in Spec-T constitutes an inherent barrier, and a TP node that dominates the subject phrase inherits barrierhood from the subject, thus constituting a barrier by inheritance.[2] The subextraction from a subject always crosses two barriers, which is a violation of the Subjacency Condition for

---

[2] Chomsky (1986a) defines "barrier" as in our term "barrierhood" in terms of "blocking category" (BC).
  (i) γ is a BC for β iff γ is not L-marked and γ dominates β.
L-marking is based on θ-marking. The definitions of L-marking and θ-marking are as follows.
  (ii) α L-marks β iff α is a lexical category that θ-governs β.
  (iii) α θ-governs β iff α is a zero-level category that θ-marks β, α, β are sisters.
The definition of "barrier" is as follows.

movement.[3] These two barriers also hinder ECP (antecedent government) from holding.[4] On the other hand, *wh*-movement from an object position never crosses a barrier, and thus there is no violation of the Subjacency Condition. ECP is also always observed in the case of *wh*-movement from objects, because of the absence of barriers.

In the early 1990s, Chomsky proposed the framework of the Minimalist Program. In this framework, some important concepts such as government, barriers, and ECP, which had played a crucial role in pre-Minimalism, were abandoned for the reason that they were not driven by conceptual necessity. Although many proposals have been made to account for the asymmetry pointed out in (1) within the Minimalist framework, the most successful proposal seems to be the one by Chomsky (2008) using the Inactivity Condition and the Locality Condition (as we will see in detail in the next chapter). However, closer inspection of the data on subextraction of a *wh*-phrase out of a subject reveals that there are phenomena that Chomsky's (2008) analysis cannot deal with. The primary purpose of this book is to give a principled account to such phenomena and to propose a comprehensive theory that can explain asymmetry between subjects and objects within the framework of Minimalism.

1.2. General Framework

This book adopts as its theoretical framework the Minimalist Program developed by Chomsky (1993, 1995, 2000, 2001, 2004, 2006, 2008). In this introductory section, I will first introduce a set of concepts adopted in Minimalist theory that are minimally necessary for understanding the discussion in the following chapters.

(iv) γ is a barrier for β iff (a) and (b):
    a. γ immediately dominates δ, δ a BC for β;
    b. γ is a BC for β, $\gamma \neq$ IP

[3] We assume 1-subjacency for the Subjacency Condition.
    (i) β is n-subjacent to α iff there are fewer than n+1 barriers for β that exclude α.
"Exclusion" in (i) is as follows.
    (ii) α excludes β if no segment of α dominates β.
    As to the definition of "exclusion," see May (1977, 1985).

[4] ECP requires that traces be properly governed. As for "proper government," we assume here with Chomsky (1986: 88) that proper-government is antecedent-government.

1.2.1. The Model of Grammar

We assume the general architecture of the language faculty proposed by Chomsky (2001, 2004, 2006, 2008), according to which, Language has three components: Narrow Syntax; the phonological component, Φ; and the semantic component, Σ.

A derivation begins with a set of lexical items on which syntactic operations such as Agree and Merge are carried out to form syntactic objects. We will see examples of these syntactic operations in 1.2.3 and 1.2.4. Each lexical item, which we assume consists of a bundle of features (see next subsection), is drawn from the Lexicon. A set of lexical items drawn from the Lexicon forms a Lexical Array (LA). For instance, the LA for the sentence in (6a) is (6b).

(6) a. We build an airplane.
    b. LA: {we, build, an airplane, C, T, v*}

Notice here that, as claimed above, each lexical item consists of a bundle of features that are realized together as a word by virtue of Late Vocabulary Insertion, in the sense of Distributed Morphology. The LA is extended to Numeration if information on the number of times that a lexical item is selected is added. Taking Citko's (2014) account as an example, consider (7). Here, functional categories as well as two lexical categories are added. Thus, we have (7c) as the Numeration of (7a).

(7) a. They think we build an airplane.
    b. LA: {they, think, we, build, an airplane, C, T, v}
    c. Numeration: {they$_1$, think$_1$, we$_1$, build$_1$, an$_1$, airplane$_1$, C$_2$, T$_2$, v$_2$}

We assume that a lexical item is selected by the operation "Select" to form syntactic objects, and that in order for a derivation to converge, all lexical items in the LA must be exhausted or the subscript number added to each lexical item in Numeration must be reduced to 0.

Suppose that in the course of the derivation of (6a), a syntactic object *We build an airplane* is formed by operations such as Select, Agree, and Merge (or Move). The output that we get is a pair of representations <PHON, SEM> of (6a). These two representations are accessed by the Sensorimotor (S-M) system and the Conceptual-Intentional (C-I) system, respectively. Conditions imposed by these two systems are called "Interface Conditions." We follow Chomsky's Strong Minimalist Thesis (SMT), as in (8).

(8) [...] language is an optimal solution to interface conditions that FL [Faculty of Language, H.E.] must satisfy; that is, language is an optimal way to link sound and meaning [...]   (Chomsky (2008: 135))

This, in turn, implies that a pair of representations <PHON, SEM> of a derived syntactic object consists of features that Interface Conditions can interpret; otherwise, the derivation crashes.

From the discussion above, we get the following model of the grammar of language.

(9)
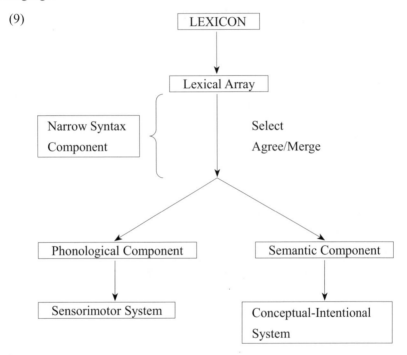

1.2.2. Features

Following subsequent work in the framework of Minimalism by Chomsky, we assume that both lexical and functional items drawn from the lexicon consist of a bundle of features. As to the nature or types of these features, we follow the framework of Chomsky (1995), who argues that both lexical and functional items have three kinds of features: phonological, semantic, and formal features. Taking a lexical item *airplane* as an example, he claims that it contains phonological feature such as [begin with vowel], semantic features such as [artifact], and formal features such as [nominal]. Among these three types of features, formal features are particularly important, in that they play a crucial role in the derivation, in the narrow syntax.

Let us now look at the formal features of a noun phrase in detail. It is assumed that all nouns have case features such as [NOM(inative)], [ACC(usative)] and so on and φ-features (or Agreement features) [person], [number], and [gender].[5] Consider the nouns in the following sentence.

(10) We built an airplane.

In (10) two noun expressions appear; one is the pronoun *we* in the subject position and the other is *airplane* in the object position. The φ-features of *we* are [2nd person] and [plural], and those of *airplane* are [3rd person] and [singular]. The φ-feature values of individual nouns are specified in the lexicon and interpretable at the C-I interface. Thus, *we* and *airplane* in (10) have the following formal features.[6]

(11) *we*: φ-features ([2nd person], [+plural]), case feature: [...]
      airplane: φ-features ([3rd person], [−plural]), case feature [...]

Notice here that a noun also has an unvalued case feature, which is shown as [...]. This unvalued case feature is uninterpretable because the value is not given within the structure of the noun itself. The valuation of the case feature takes place under agreement with a functional category. We will see how the case feature is valued in the next subsection.

It is worth noticing here that (10) also contains such abstract functional categories as C(omplementizer), T(ense), and v* (a transitive light verb). Let us concentrate on the formal features of T. (We will see the formal features of C and v* in detail later.) T in (10) contains tense feature [+Past], and the φ-features corresponding to the subject *we*.[7] However, contrary to the φ-features of the subject, the values of the φ-features of T are unspecified (or unvalued); and if they remain unvalued, uninterpretable features will be sent to the phonological component and/or the semantic component. They need to be valued in the course of the derivation; otherwise the derivation will crash, as in the case of (10). We will take up the matter of φ-feature valuation in the 1.2.3. In (10), in this case a finite T, also has

---

[5] We will leave out the feature [gender] for the sake of exposition because in English [gender] is not salient.
[6] We adopt the notation of [±plural] for number.
[7] As to the origin of the formal features of T, see the discussion in 1.2.3.

a case feature [NOM], which is uninterpretable and has to be deleted in the course of derivation. Thus, T in (10) has the following formal features.

(12) T: [+Past], [uφ] (α person, α plural), [NOM][8]

We have seen that lexical and functional items (or categories) are drawn from the lexicon as feature bundles, and observed their featural constitution. In the next subsection, we will see how these features interact through the derivation of a sentence.

1.2.3. Agree

Following Citko (2014), who sums up Agree Conditions on the basis of Chomsky (2000), we assume that the following four conditions must be met in order for Agree to hold.

(13) a. The Activity Condition
    The Probe and Goal have to be active, where being active means having uninterpretable/unvalued features.
  b. The Matching Condition
    The features of the Probe and Goal have to match, where matching refers to feature identity.
  c. The Domain Condition
    The Goal has to be inside the domain of the Probe, where the domain of the Probe is its sister.
  d. The Locality Condition
    The Goal has to be in a local relationship, where locality is closest c-command.[9] (Citko (2014: 20–21))

Suppose we have the following structure, where T has unvalued φ-features, represented as [uφ], and case feature [NOM], which is uninterpretable, and where the DP generated in Spec-v* has both a valued [φ] and an unvalued case feature, represented as [...].[10]

---

[8] The notation "u" in [uφ] means "unvalued." α in (3) means an unspecified value; α of person ranges from 1st to 3rd and α of plural is either + or −.
[9] We follow the traditional definition of c-command.
  (i) α c-commands β iff α does not dominate β and every γ that dominates α dominates β.
[10] The φ-features assumed here are [person] and [number].

(14)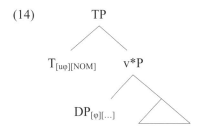

In (14) all the conditions in (13) are satisfied: a probe T and a goal DP are active, because they have unvalued/uninterpretable features: features of T and DP match, since they have φ-features and a case feature in common: a goal DP is inside the sister of a probe T; and the goal DP is c-commanded by the closest probe T. As a result, the unvalued [uφ] of T is valued, represented as [ʉφ], and the unvalued case feature of DP is valued as [NOM].[11]

(15) a.   T: [uφ] [NOM]   DP: [uφ] […]
     b.   T: [ʉφ] [NOM]   DP: [uφ] [NOM]

We will see in 1.2.6 how φ-features are given values by the Agree operation in 1.2.5.

1.2.4. Merge

Before Chomsky (2004), it was considered that the (pure) Merge operation is more economical than the Move operation. The Move operation gives rise to the "displacement" property of human language, which is a peculiar property but one that is ubiquitous among languages. Generative Grammar from the perspective of the framework of the Minimalist Program has to explain the displacement property; otherwise Generative Grammar does not conform to the SMT in (10) above. Given this state of affairs, Chomsky (2004) reexamines the Move operation and makes an attempt to reduce it to the Merge operation. He argues that there are two types of Merge operation, namely, External Merge (EM) and Internal Merge (IM). EM takes independent elements α and β from the Lexical Array and combines them to form a new syntactic element, as demonstrated below.

---

[11] We should note here that we will propose in Chapter 2 a different mechanism of case assignment: case assignment under Merge.

(16) a. α   b.

In contrast, IM takes α and a part of β and extends β by combining α with it, as shown in (17).

(17) a.   b.
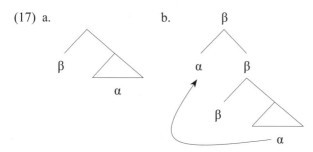

In contrast to (16a), α and β are in the same structure in (17a), whereas (17b) is derived by the (Internal) Merge operation of α to β, as a result of which α becomes a part of β. Notice here that two occurrences of α in (17b) are copies. Therefore, the derived structure is the same as the structure derived from the Move operation; in other words, IM yields the same outcome as the Move operation does. Viewed in this way, IM as a subtype of the Merge operation opens up a new way to analyze the "displacement" property as not peculiar but natural. This shift in perspective leads to the conclusion that the movement operation recaptured by IM conforms to SMT.

This perspective has another consequence. As noted above, the (pure) Merge operation has been considered more economical than the Move operation. However, if the Move operation is a subtype of the Merge operation, it is not the case that it is less economical than the (pure) Merge operation. This is explicitly stated in Chomsky (2014).

(18) *IM* is simpler, since it requires vastly less search than *EM* (*which must access the workspace of already generated objects and the lexicon*). (Chomsky (2013: 41))

Even though I will be using the terms "move/movement" and "attract/attraction" in this book mostly for familiarity's sake, I assume that "internal merge" holds throughout.

1.2.5. Bare Phrase Structure

Chomsky (1995) proposes the Inclusiveness Condition, which states that any structure built by computation must consist only of elements already present among the lexical items selected for Lexical Array/Numeration. With this condition in mind, let us examine the phrase structure of (19).

(19) We will build an airplane.

According to the traditional phrase structure representation, (19) has the following structure.

(20)

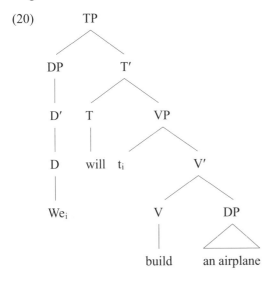

In traditional X-bar theory, the subject pronoun *we* is the projection of D, while T and V project intermediate projections T′ and V′, which in turn project TP and VP. The subject *we* is generated in Spec-V, from which it is raised to Spec-T, leaving behind its trace, represented as *t*, and the same index is given to *we* and *t*. However, the representation above does not conform to the Inclusiveness Condition. There are items that are not present in the Lexical Array or Numeration—the bar notations found in D′, T′, and V′ are among them. The notation of *t* standing for a trace and the subscript "i" added to *we* and *t* are not items from the lexical array; they are added in the course of derivation. Chomsky (1994) argues that these problems can be avoided by adoption of Bare Phrase Structure, and the Copy Theory of movement. We will focus on Bare Phrase Structure here and will discuss the Copy Theory in detail in 2.3.1 from the perspective of Overt Syntax Hypothesis. Bare Phrase Structure enables us to remove redundant items from the representation in (20).

(21)
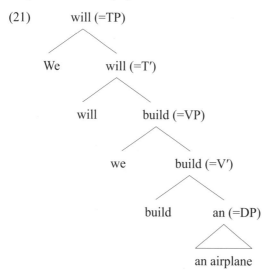

In (21), bar notations, *t*(race), and indices are eliminated completely, and yet the information that the prediction of traditional X-bar theory yields can also be gained through Bare Phrase Structure, in terms of the relative position that an item occupies. For instance, *will* is a minimal projection, and forms a larger constituent with *build* (=VP) by taking it as its complement; and this larger constituent forms a maximal projection *will* (=TP) by hosting a raised subject in its specifier position. The same is true of VP.

Although I will be adopting the notation of traditional X-bar theory in this book for expository convenience, I make the theoretical assumption that Bare Phrase Structure holds throughout.

1.2.6. Derivation

Following Chomsky (2001, 2004, 2007, 2008), we assume that the derivation of an expression proceeds phase by phase. A phase is a syntactic unit headed by a phase head. All operations have to be completed at the phase level; when this is done, the (complement) domain of a phase head undergoes the "Transfer" operation. Transfer hands a syntactic unit generated in the narrow syntax to the phonological component and the semantic component. Chomsky further maintains that in English, v* and C are phase heads (where v* is a light verb that heads a transitive VP). These heads have uninterpretable features that feed computation.

Now let us see how the sentence in (21) is generated under the Phase Theory proposed by Chomsky (2008).

(22)   We build an airplane.

In the v*P phase, we have (23), where a transitive v* takes VP as its complement, hosting a subject in its Spec.

(23)

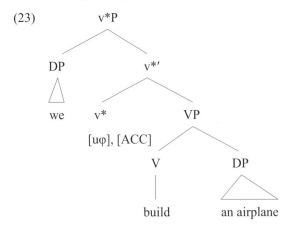

We assume with Chomsky (2008) that a transitive v* has the case feature [ACC] and unvalued φ-features corresponding to those of the object, and that V inherits these features.[12] Agreement holds between V and the object, and as a result, the previously unvalued features of V become valued, as seen in (24) below.

(24)   V ◄──── AGREEMENT ────► airplane
       uφ-features (α person, α plural)   φ-features ([3rd person],
       uφ-features (3rd person, −plural)   [−plural])

The φ-features of V attracts the object to its Spec, in which the unvalued case feature [...] of the noun becomes valued as [ACC], with the main verb V (*build*) raising to v*.

---

[12] Although Chomsky considers [ACC] to be assigned to the object DP as a reflex of the agreement holding between the DP and V, we assume that v* and the object take [ACC] and [...], respectively. See the discussion in 1.2.2 for details.

(25)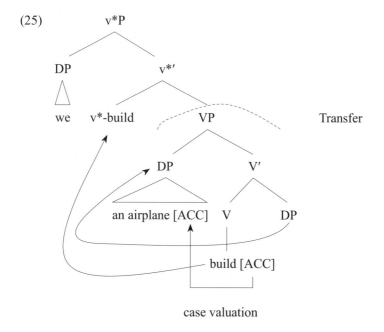

At this point, all the operations apply, as a result of which the VP undergoes the Transfer operation.

In the next stage of the derivation, the CP phase, C and T are merged to v*P, represented in (26). At this stage, the same processes take place as happened in the v*P phase.

(26)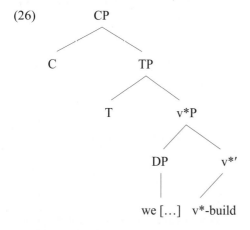

As argued in the previous section, 1.2.2, T has three kinds of formal features: [−Past], uφ-features (α person, α plural), and [NOM]. These features do not belong to T originally; rather, phase head C has these features and T inherits them. This is the same operation that we have seen in v*P phase: uninterpretable φ-features and the case feature originate in v*, which is a phase head, and V inherits them. The agreement between T and the subject in Spec-v* holds, as seen in (27).

(27) T ←——— AGREEMENT ———→ we
      uφ-features (α person, α plural)   φ-features ([2nd person],
      uφ-features (2nd person, +plural)   [+plural])

The φ-features that of T has raised the subject in Spec-v* to Spec-T, where T values the unvalued case feature [...] of the subject as [NOM].

(28)

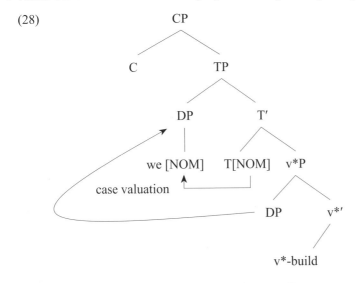

All the operations are completed in (28); the overall structure undergoes the Transfer operation and is sent to the phonological component and the semantic component.

The derivation shown above is crucially different from those in previous analyses in terms of its treatment of the object of a verb. Although it was widely accepted that the object of a verb does not move in English, in Phase Theory it is raised to Spec-V for case-theoretic reasons as seen in (28) above. This analysis captures the facts concerning ECM (Exceptional Case Marking) constructions, which were pointed out by Postal (1974) and Lasnik and Saito (1991). Before showing the consequences of object-raising, let us review the analysis of the ECM constructions briefly. From the early era of Generative Grammar to the early Minimalism era, and up until Chomsky (2008), it was considered that an ECM verb takes TP as its complement while the subject (or the object of the ECM verb) stays in Spec-T, where the subject is case-assigned exceptionally by the matrix verb. For instance, according to GB analysis, the ECM construction in (29a) has such a structure as (29b).

(29) a. The DA proved the defendants to be guilty.
b. The DA proved [$_{TP}$ the defendants to be guilty].

In (29) the matrix verb *proved* governs *the defendants* in Spec-T across the node TP, which is not a barrier and thus transparent for government from outside.[13] Therefore, the embedded subject "the defendant" can be case-assigned. However, this analysis cannot predict the (un)grammaticality of the following sentences.

(30) a. *John believes him$_i$ to be a genius [even more fervently than Bob$_i$ does].
b. The DA proved the defendants$_i$ to be guilty [during each other's$_i$ trials]. (Lasnik and Saito 1991: 328–329)

(30a) is ungrammatical in the interpretation in which *him* corefers with *Bob*, and (30b) is grammatical under the interpretation in which *defendants* corefers with *each other*. In other words, while (30a) violates Binding Condition (C), (30b) observes Binding Condition (A). These binding facts in (30) suggest that the ECM subject is higher than a bracketed adjunct phrase. This cannot be predicted under the analysis in which the ECM subject stays in Spec-T, together with the assumption that the bracketed adjunct phrase in (29) is adjoined to the verb phrase that the ECM verb heads, because the ECM subjects do not c-command either the R-expression *Bob* or the reciprocal pronoun *each other*.

---

[13] On the transparency of TP, see the definition of *barrier* in footnote 2.

Chapter 1 Goals and Framework 17

(31)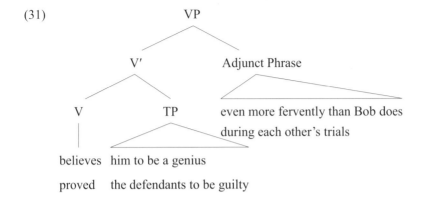

However, the object-raising analysis shown in (25) does correctly predict the (un)grammaticality of (30). In the v*P phase of (30), we have (32).

(32)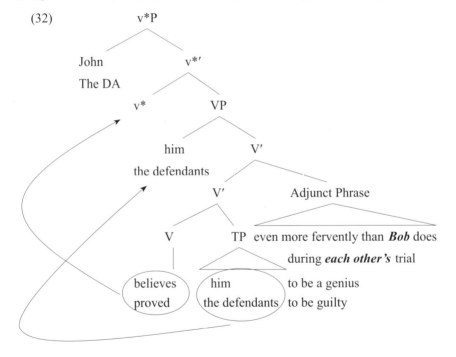

As argued in (25), the main verb inherits unvalued φ-features and the case feature [ACC] from the phase head v*, with φ-feature agreement holding between the main verb and the ECM subject. The φ-features of V raise the ECM subject to its Spec, where the ECM subject's unvalued case feature becomes valued as [ACC], with the main verb raised to v*. In (32) the raised object (the ECM subject) c-commands the r-expression *Bob* and the reciprocal expression *each other*. We can conclude from the binding facts observed in (30) that the object of an ECM verb (the ECM subject) undergoes the movement operation to Spec-V.

Before leaving this section, we should observe the derivation of a *wh*-interrogative sentence, as in (33) below.

(33) Who do you see?

In the v*P phase v* has Edge Feature [EF] as well as the case feature [ACC] and uφ-features of the object. As observed above, the main verb (*see*) inherits the uφ-features and [ACC] from v*, with agreement holding between V and the object DP, and the object is raised to the Spec-V, where its unvalued case feature becomes valued as [ACC]. The main verb is raised to v*.

(34)

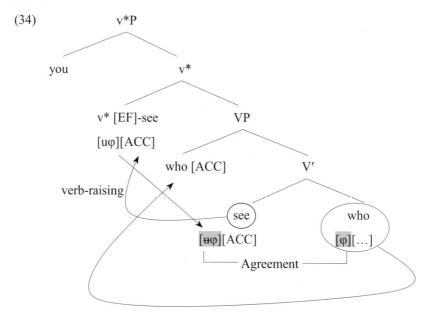

Notice here that the phase head v* still has [EF]. This [EF] functions as a probe and locates two copies of a *wh*-phrase, one in Spec-v* and the other in the complement of V. Chomsky (2008) argues that the Inactivity Condition as given in (35) below prohibits the *wh*-phrase in Spec-V from being raised.[14]

(35) Inactivity Condition
The head of an A-chain becomes invisible to further computation when its uninterpretable features are valued. (Chomsky (2008: 150))

In (34) the *wh*-phrase in Spec-V is the head of an A-chain, and an unvalued feature, in this example the case feature [ACC], becomes valued. This means that *who* in Spec-V is invisible to further computation. Then, v*'s [EF] raises the *wh*-phrase in the complement position of the verb. This *wh*-phrase is still active because its uninterpretable feature, in this case unvalued case feature […], is not valued.

(36)

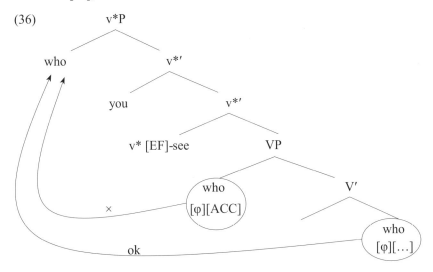

It is worth noticing here that A-movement of the *wh*-phrase (the movement to Spec-V) and A'-movement of the *wh*-phrase (the movement to Spec-v*) take place in parallel or simultaneously. At this point the v*P phase is completed and the VP, which is the domain of v*, undergoes the Transfer operation.

In the matrix CP phase, C with [EF] as well as [uφ] and [NOM], and T are introduced, with T inheriting [uφ] and [NOM] from C, and the subject *you* is raised to Spec-T by virtue of the [uφ] that T has, where the unvalued

---

[14] Originally, this condition was proposed in order to exclude subextraction of a *wh*-phrase from Spec-T. See the next chapter for details.

case feature [...] that the subject has is valued as [NOM]. T (*do*) is also raised to C. These agreement relations are presented in (37a), and the derived structure is in (37b).

(37) a. T ←——— AGREEMENT ———→ you
    uφ (α person, α plural) [NOM]   φ ([2nd person], [−plural]) [...]
    uφ (2nd person, −plural) [NOM]   φ ([2nd person], [−plural]) [NOM]

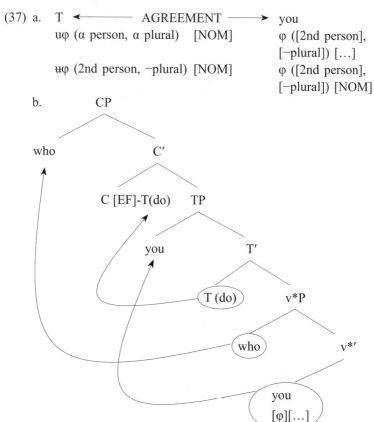

Notice that these complex operations all take place at the same time, in the CP phase. Once all these operations are completed, the overall structure undergoes the Transfer operation.

In this section, we have reviewed how Chomsky's (2008) Phase Theory works. In the next chapter, we will observe how the Phase Theory deals with the Subject Condition, point out some empirical problems with Chomsky's analysis, and propose an alternative analysis.

Chapter 2

On the Subject Condition

2.1. Phase-Based Approach to the Subject Condition

Since the proposal of Minimalism by Chomsky in the early 1990s, many attempts have been made in the framework of the Minimalist Program to account for ungrammaticality caused by violation of the Subject Condition, as observed in (1).[1]

(1) *Of which car did [the (driver, picture) cause a scandal]?

(Chomsky (2008: 147))

The most successful account so far seems to me to be the one by Chomsky (2008), based on Phase Theory. In this section, we will briefly examine this "phase-based approach" to the Subject Condition.

In the v*P phase of (1), we have (2), where the head of the VP (*cause*) undergoes head-movement to v* and the subject *the driver of which car* is merged to Spec-v*.

(2) [$_{v*P}$ the driver of which car [$_{v*'}$ [$_{v*}$ cause] [$_{VP}$ the scandal]]]

Once all the operations that apply in this phase have been completed, the domain of v* (i.e. the VP complement) undergoes the Transfer operation. In the next stage of the derivation, C and T are merged to the structure in (2). C in (3) has an edge feature [EF], unvalued φ-features, and the case

---

[1] See 1.1 for details on the Subject Condition.

feature [NOM].

(3) [$_{CP}$ C$_{[EF]}$ $_{[u\varphi][NOM]}$ [$_{TP}$ T [$_{v*P}$ the driver of which car$_{[...]}$ [$_{v*'}$ [$_{v*}$ cause] [$_{VP}$ ~~the scandal~~]]]]][2]

In (3), C$_{[EF]}$ finds the *wh*-phrase in Spec-v* and raises it to Spec-C. On the other hand, uninterpretable φ-features [uφ] and the case feature [NOM] are inherited by T, as a result of which, the agreement relation holds between T and the subject DP in Spec-v* with respect to φ-features, with the subject DP in v*P raised to Spec-T, where the unvalued case feature [...] of the subject is valued as [NOM]. Notice here that these operations proceed in parallel or simultaneously.

(4)

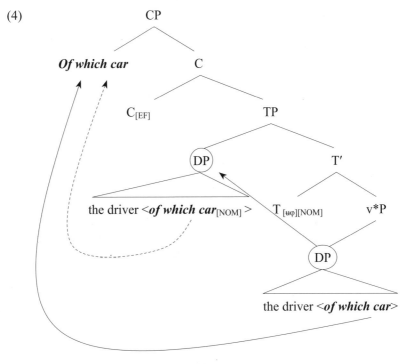

As indicated by the ungrammaticality of (1), *wh*-movement from Spec-v* to the matrix Spec-C must be excluded. Chomsky argues that *wh*-extraction from Spec-v* causes the violation of the Locality Condition (henceforth LC): C$_{[EF]}$ in (4) cannot access the *wh*-phrase in Spec-v* because the latter is em-

---

[2] Throughout, phrases undergoing the Transfer operation are marked with strikethrough.

bedded in the lower phase, which has already been passed in the derivation; he further argues that there is a cost to extracting it. However, there is another possible *wh*-movement that should be excluded, namely, *wh*-movement from Spec-T, as represented by the dotted line in (4) above. According to Chomsky (2008: 150), *wh*-extraction from Spec-T is prohibited by the Inactivity Condition (henceforth IC).

(5) Inactivity Condition
The head of an A-chain becomes invisible to further computation when its uninterpretable features are valued.
(Chomsky (2008: 150))

The subject DP in Spec-T in (4) is the head of an A-chain, and its uninterpretable (unvalued) feature—here, the case feature [NOM]—is valued; thus, the whole DP is invisible to further computation. Thus, the [EF] of C cannot attract the *wh*-phrase in the subject DP. This is the phase-based approach to the Subject Condition. As we have seen, this explanation depends on the LC, which prohibits extraction from the Spec of a phase head, and on the IC, which prohibits extraction from the head of an A-chain.

Chomsky supports his analysis with the following sentences.

(6) *Of which car did you wonder [which (picture, driver) [caused a scandal]] (Chomsky (2008: 153))

(7) a. Of which car is [the (driver, picture) likely [t to [t cause a scandal]]] (ibid.)
b. Of which car did they believe the (driver, picture) to have caused a scandal (ibid.)

Above, (6) involves subextraction of a *wh*-phrase from a larger *wh*-phrase that has moved into the embedded Spec-C, and its grammaticality is degraded. In contrast, (7a) and (7b) involve subextraction from the raised subject and the raised object (the ECM subject), respectively, and the grammaticality is not degraded.

Let us first examine (6). At an early stage of the derivation, we have (8), where the complex *wh*-expression *which (picture, driver) of which car* moves to the embedded Spec-C, with TP, which is the complement domain of the embedded $C_{[EF]}$, transferred; and the matrix v* is merged with the matrix VP to form v*P, to whose specifier position and head position the subject *you* and the main verb *wonder* are merged, respectively.

(8) [$_{v*P}$ you [$_{v*'}$ [$_{v*}$ wonder$_{[EF]}$][$_{VP}$ ___ [$_{CP}$ which (picture, driver) of which car [$_{C'}$ C$_{[EF]}$ [~~TP caused the scandal~~]]]]]

Notice here that the matrix v* (*wonder*) is a phase head and has [EF]. This matrix v*, however, cannot attract the *wh*-phrase *which car* in the embedded Spec-C because the *wh*-phrase is embedded in the lower phase, that is, in the embedded CP, which has already passed in the derivation; thus, such an attraction would lead to violation of the LC. The explanation here is thus the same as that for the Subject Condition discussed above: prohibition of subextraction from a subject embedded in Spec-v*. Claiming that (6) and (1) both have the same ungrammatical status, Chomsky argues on this basis that (6) lends support to his analysis of the LC.

Before turning to (7), let us briefly review the discussion on prohibition of subextraction from Spec-T. As we have seen, according to the IC, subextraction from Spec-T is impossible if uninterpretable features are valued in that position. This predicts that subextraction from Spec-T is possible as long as uninterpretable features are not valued in this position. With this prediction in mind, let us now consider (7). In the early stage of the derivation, the two sentences in (7) have the following structure in common, wherein the subject is generated in Spec-v* and the domain of v*, VP, is transferred.

(9) [$_{v*P}$ the driver of which car [$_{v*'}$ v*-cause /v*-have caused [~~VP the scandal~~]]]

In the next stage of the derivation, an infinitival *to* that has the [EPP] (Extended Projection Principle) feature is merged to form TP, to whose specifier position the subject *the driver of which car* is raised.

(10) [$_{TP}$ the driver of which car [$_{T'}$ [$_T$ to$_{[EPP]}$] [$_{v*P}$ the driver of which car [$_{v*'}$ v*-cause / v*-have caused]]]

The two sentences in (7) have in common the same derivations, shown in (9) and (10). From here we will first see the derivation of (7a), and see that of (7b) later. In the next stage of the derivation of (7a), the raising predicate *likely* and *be* are merged.[3]

---

[3] The raising predicate in (11) consists of VP and AP. Irrelevant structure is omitted here for convenience.

(11) [$_{VP}$ be likely [$_{TP}$ the driver of which car [$_{T'}$ [$_T$ to$_{[EPP]}$] [$_{v*P}$ the driver of which car

Here, C, with [EF], unvalued φ-features [uφ], and the case feature [NOM], and T are merged to (11), with T inheriting [uφ] and [NOM], triggering Internal Merge of the subject to Spec-T.[4, 5]

(12) [$_{CP}$ C$_{[EF]}$ [$_{TP}$ the driver of which car [$_{T'}$ T$_{[uφ]}$ is [$_{VP}$ likely [$_{TP}$ the driver of which car [$_{T'}$ [$_T$ to$_{[EPP]}$] [$_{v*P}$ the driver of which car]]]]]]]

As argued in 1.2.3, an unvalued case feature [...] that the subject DP has is valued as [NOM] in Spec-T. The matrix C with [EF] functions as a Probe and locates three possible *wh*-phrases as candidates for attraction to its Spec: the one in the matrix Spec-T, that in the embedded Spec-T, and that in Spec-v*. The *wh*-movement from the matrix Spec-T and that from the embedded Spec-v* are excluded by the IC and the LC, respectively, as discussed above: the unvalued case feature of the subject DP in the matrix Spec-T has is valued and thus invisible to further computation, while the predicate internal subject DP is embedded in the lower phase that has already been passed in the derivation. Thus, the remaining candidate for *wh*-attraction is from the embedded Spec-T (*to*).

At this point we need to discuss the status of infinitival T. According to Bošković (1996, 1997), Chomsky (2001), Chomsky and Lasnik (1995), Martin (2001), and Stowell (1982), among others, there are two types of infinitival T (*to*). Observe the data in (13) below, which contain an infinitival T.

(13) a. John tried [PRO to enjoy Hawaii].
  b. John$_i$ seems [t$_i$ to enjoy Hawaii].
  c. John believes her$_i$ [t$_i$ to enjoy Hawaii]

Above, (13a) is a control structure, and its infinitival T (*to*) checks the null case of PRO.[6] This means that the infinitival T has a complete set of (unvalued) φ-features (that is, it is "φ-complete," in the sense of Chomsky (2001)). Null case is assigned to PRO under the Agreement holding between PRO, which also has corresponding valued φ-features, and the in-

---

[4] We implicitly assume that [uφ] is valued, in terms of Agreement holding between T and the subject. Regarding Agreement, see the discussion in 1.2.6 for details.
[5] We implicitly assume that *be* is raised to T and agrees with the subject.
[6] As for Null Case Theory, see Bošković (1996, 1997), Chomsky and Lasnik (1995), and Martin (2001), among others.

finitival *to*. On the other hand, (b) and (c) in (13) are raising constructions: (13b) is a subject-raising construction and (13c) an object-raising construction (or the ECM (Exceptional Case Marking) construction).[7] The infinitival T (*to*) of these constructions does not contain a complete set of φ features (that is, it is φ-defective in the sense of Chomsky (2001)),[8] and therefore it cannot value the unvalued case feature that DP has. This φ-defectiveness of raising T enables the DP to continue moving to where it should be because the DP is still visible to further computation due to the fact that its case feature is not valued.

(14) a. [$_{TP}$ John seems [$_{TP}$ John T(to) [visit Hawaii]]]

b. John believes [$_{VP}$ her V [$_{TP}$ her [$_{T'}$ T(to) [enjoy Hawaii]]]][9]

With this property of infinitival raising T in mind, let us turn to the derivation of ((12)=7a, repeated here as (15) below), where the matrix C, with [EF], [uφ] and [NOM], and T are merged to the matrix VP already formed.

(15) [$_{CP}$ C$_{[EF][u\varphi][NOM]}$ [$_{TP}$ T [$_{VP}$ is likely [$_{TP}$ the driver of which car [$_{T'}$ [$_{T}$ to$_{[EPP]}$] [$_{v*P}$ the driver of which car]]]]]]

In (15), C's [EF] attracts the *wh*-phrase *of which car* from the embedded Spec-T, and the matrix T that inherits [uφ] and [NOM] from C attracts the DP *the driver of which car* from the embedded Spec-T.

---

[7] As to the structure and derivation of the object-raising construction, see 1.2.6 for details.
[8] Chomsky (2001) argues that these T's are defective in that they only contain the [person] feature.
[9] In object-raising constructions, the matrix V has a complete set of φ-features, inherited from the matrix v*.

(16)

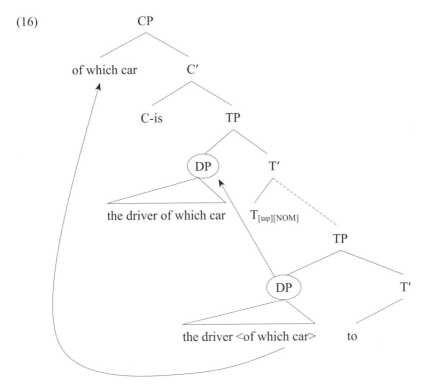

It is worth noting here that the movement of the *wh*-phrase *of which car* from the embedded Spec-T does not violate the IC because, as argued above, the raising T (*to*) is φ-defective and thus cannot value unvalued case features of the subject DP.

Now let us turn to (7b), repeated here as (17).

(17) Of which car did they believe the (driver, picture) to have caused a scandal?

The same explanation can be applied to (17). Suppose that the derivation of (17) proceeds to (18), where the object DP *the driver of which car* is attracted to the embedded Spec-T from the embedded Spec-v* and where [EF], the unvalued φ-features, and the case feature [ACC] are assigned to the matrix v*, and the matrix subject is merged to Spec-v*.[10]

---

[10] For the derivation of the embedded TP, see (10) above.

(18) [$_{v*P}$ they [$_{v*'}$ v*$_{[EF][u\varphi][ACC]}$ [$_{VP}$ expect [$_{TP}$ the driver of which car [$_{T'}$ to [$_{vP}$ have caused a scandal]]]]]]

The feature inheritance of [uφ] and [ACC] from v* to V (*expect*) takes place, and thereby the [uφ][11] that V (*expect*) inherits attracts the object DP *the driver of which car* to Spec-V, where the case feature of the object DP is valued as [ACC]. At the same time, the [EF] of v* attracts a *wh*-phrase *of which car*:

(19)

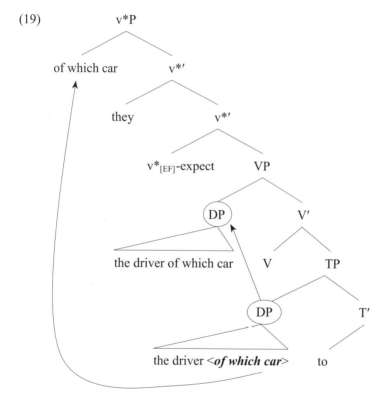

There are two possible *wh*-extractions, from two positions: one from the DP in Spec-V and the other from the one in Spec-T. However, *wh*-extraction from Spec-V is impossible because of the IC: as argued above, the unvalued case feature is valued in this position. On the other hand, *wh*-extraction from the infinitival Spec-T does not violate the IC because, as argued above,

---

[11] The unvalued φ-features are valued by means of the fact that Agree holds between V (*expect*) and its object.

object-raising T (*to*) is φ-defective and cannot value the unvalued case feature of the object DP. This, in turn, means that the *wh*-phrase can successfully be subextracted from the position without causing violation of the IC.

To summarize this section, we have seen how the LC and the IC interact with subextraction from Spec-v* and Spec-T. We have also seen that subextraction is possible from Spec-T as long as the IC is observed. In other words, these two conditions can predict the (un)grammaticality of Subject Condition violations. In the next section, we will see other cases of the Subject Condition and show that phase-based explanation of the Subject Condition cannot deal with these cases.

2.2. Some Problems

In the previous section we have seen that ungrammaticality caused by the violation of the Subject Condition can be accounted for in terms of the LC and the IC. However, a closer inspection of other data containing subextraction of a *wh*-phrase from a subject reveals that there is a grammatical counterexample, which a phase-based analysis depending on the IC and LC cannot deal with. Observe the following grammatical sentence, (20) below.

(20) Of which major is it important for the students to take a course in physics?[12]

In (20), the *wh*-phrase undergoes subextraction from the infinitival subject, but its grammaticality is not degraded. As is widely accepted, the infinitival lexical subject is case-marked by the prepositional complementizer *for*. This means that the IC excludes (20) as ungrammatical, which is not the case.

Now let us see in detail how the phase-based approach to the analyzes (20). We will first analyze the infinitival clause with a lexical subject in (21) in the framework of Phase Theory.

(21) It is important [for them to take a course in physics].

We assume with Radford (2009) that in an embedded CP phase, the infinitival complementizer *for* is introduced with a complete set of unvalued φ-features [uφ] and the case feature [ACC], and that the infinitival T (*to*) inherits these features—as demonstrated in (22), below. We also assume that the infinitival subject has valued φ-features [φ] and an unvalued case feature

---

[12] I owe the judgment of (20) to Eloise Pearson (p.c.) and Michael Farquharson (p.c.).

[…].

(22) [$_{CP}$ for~~[uφ][ACC]~~ [$_{TP}$ to$_{[uφ][ACC]}$ [$_{v*P}$ him$_{[φ][...]}$ v*-take ~~[$_{VP}$ a course in physics]~~]]]

As a result of inheritance of these features, T serves as a probe and locates the subject *him* in Spec-v*, and as a result, the unvalued φ-features of T are valued. Furthermore, T's [uφ] attracts the infinitival subject from Spec-v* to Spec-T, where the unvalued case feature […] of the subject is valued as [ACC].

(23) [$_{CP}$ for [$_{TP}$ him$_{[ACC]}$ [$_{T'}$ to$_{[uφ][ACC]}$ [$_{v*P}$ him v*-take ~~[$_{VP}$ a course in physics]~~]]]

With this derivation in mind, let us now consider (20), repeated as (24) below.

(24) Of which major is it important for the students to take a course in physics?

In the embedded CP phase, we have (25), where the infinitival complementizer *for* is introduced with [EF] as well as [uφ] and [ACC], and the latter two features are inherited by the infinitival T, as shown in (25).

(25) [$_{CP}$ for$_{[EF]}$ ~~[uφ][ACC]~~ [$_{TP}$ to$_{[uφ][ACC]}$ [$_{v*P}$ the students of which major [$_{v*'}$ v*-take]]]][13]

Here, the infinitival T serves as a probe and locates the infinitival subject *the students of which major* in Spec-v*. In consequence, T's [uφ] is valued, and this [uφ] attracts the infinitival subject from Spec-v* to Spec-T, where the unvalued case feature of the infinitival subject is then also valued, and, further, leaves a copy behind in Spec-v*.

(26) [$_{CP}$ for$_{[EF]}$ ~~[uφ][ACC]~~ [$_{TP}$ the students of which major [$_{T'}$ to$_{[uφ][ACC]}$ [$_{v*P}$ the students of which major [$_{v*'}$ v*-take]]]]]

Notice here that the [EF] of C also serves as a probe searching for a *wh*-phrase, with agreement and attraction holding between the infinitival T and the lexical subject at the same time. There are two possible goals for this probe: one in Spec-v* and the other in Spec-T.

---

[13] In (25), we implicitly assume that the most deeply embedded VP undergoes Transfer.

(27)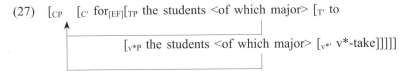
[CP [C' for[EF][TP the students <of which major> [T' to

[v*P the students <of which major> [v*' v*-take]]]]]

The attraction of a *wh*-phrase in Spec-v* is in violation of the LC: C *for*[EF] in (27) cannot access the *wh*-phrase in Spec-v* because the latter is embedded in the lower phase, which has already been passed in the derivation, and there is a cost to extracting it. The attraction of a *wh*-phrase from Spec-T, on the other hand, is a violation of the IC: the unvalued case feature […] of the infinitival subject is valued in this position. It then follows that the phase-based approach wrongly rules out (24); and so we can safely conclude that the analysis of the Subject Condition in terms of the LC and the IC wrongly excludes as ungrammatical the subextraction of a *wh*-phrase from an infinitival subject.

In fact, this is widely true of subextraction of *wh*-phrases from infinitival subjects. Let us examine (28) below.

(28) a. Of which car would you have liked (for) [the driver] to cause an accident? (Matsubara (2008: 469))
 b. Of which aspiring actress did they intend for [compromising photos] to have been sold to a national newspaper?[14]
 (Haegeman, Ángel, Fernández and Radford (2014: 79))

The same derivation can be applied to (28). Let us consider the(se) derivation(s) briefly. In the embedded CP phase, we have (29), where the infinitival T (to) inherits [uφ] and the case feature [ACC] from C and where [uφ] is valued by virtue of Agreement holding between T and the subject. This [uφ] of T attracts the infinitival subject to Spec-T, where the unvalued feature […] of the subject becomes valued as [ACC].

(29) a. [CP for[EF] [uφ][ACC] [TP the driver of which car[ACC] [T' to[uφ][ACC] [v*P the driver of which car[…]]]]]
 b. [CP for[EF] [uφ][ACC] [TP compromising photos of which aspiring actress[ACC] [T' to[uφ][ACC] [v*P compromising photos of which aspiring actress[…]]]]]

C with [EF] probes and locates two *wh*-phrases: one in Spec-v* and the

---

[14] See Matsubara (2008). He includes a similar example to (28b), which is presented by Andrew Radford.
 (i) Of which car$_i$ hadn't you intended for [the driver t_i] to cause an accident?

other in Spec-T. The attraction of the *wh*-phrase in Spec-v* leads to a violation of the LC because the *wh*-phrase is in the lower phase, and has already passed in the derivation. That from Spec-T, on the other hand, leads to a violation of the IC: the unvalued case feature of the infinitival subject is valued as [ACC], and is hence invisible to further computation. It then follows that (28) is wrongly excluded by the IC and the LC. We can safely conclude that these phenomena observed in (20) and (28) seem to cast doubt on the phase-based approach to the Subject Condition.

One might argue, against our claim, that the LC and the IC can only apply to subextraction from a subject of a finite clause, not from a subject of an infinitival clause. However, this argument cannot be borne out given the grammaticality of the following sentence, where subextraction of a *wh*-phrase takes place from the subject of the embedded finite clause.

(30) [Of which car is it likely [(that) the (driver, picture) [*t* caused a scandal]]] (Kobayashi (2009: 42))

In this section, we have reviewed Chomsky's (2008) analysis of the Subject Condition in terms of the LC and the IC. We have, further, pointed out that the account of the Subject Condition in terms of the LC and the IC cannot be retained, and demonstrated this by providing legitimate subextraction of a *wh*-phrase from an infinitival subject and also from a subject of a finite clause. Given this state of affairs, we can conclude that Chomsky's (2008) account loses its force and that some modifications of the Subject Condition are called for.

2.3. An Alternative Analysis

In this section, we will propose an alternative account of legitimate *wh*-extraction from infinitival subjects. To begin with, we will introduce as part of the basis of our account the Excorporation Analysis proposed by Tonoike (2008a, 2008c).

2.3.1. Theoretical Assumptions: The Excorporation Analysis and the Inactivity Condition

As observed in Chapter 1, since Chomsky (2000, 2001, 2004, 2007, 2008), the derivation of a sentence proceeds by "phase." The analysis of "phase" is based on the idea that the Language Faculty can only process limited amounts of linguistic structure at one time, and can only hold limited amounts of structure in its active memory. Chomsky argues that this notion of phase helps ensure a reduction of computational burden. Chomsky (2008) further elaborates this Phase Theory by proposing that Internal Merge (or the movement operation) be driven by a phase head, which we assume here to be C and v*.

However, this concept seems to introduce some complications in the grammar. One such complication concerns the notion of feature inheritance. In the derivation of the v*P phase of the sentence in (31a) below, unvalued φ-features [uφ] and the case feature are originally assigned to v*.

(31) a. We build an airplane.
b. [$_{v*P}$ we [$_{v*'}$ v*$_{[uφ][ACC]}$ [$_{VP}$ build an airplane]]]

As discussed in Chapter 1, these features are inherited by V, as seen in (32).

(32)

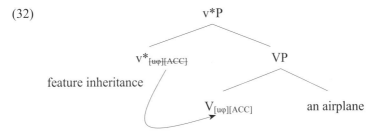

As pointed out by Tonoike (2008a, b), this operation is obviously a lowering operation, a type of operation that Generative Grammar, including the Minimalist Program, has been seeking to eliminate.

Another complication arises with respect to the Extension Condition. Suppose that the derivation of (32) proceeds to (33), where the object *an airplane* raises to Spec-V for case-theoretic reasons, and the main verb (*build*) undergoes head-movement to v*.

(33)

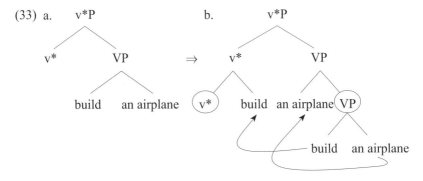

These two raising operations do not extend the categories that they target, which is in violation of the Extension Condition, as given in (34)

(34) The Extension Condition
GT and Move α [must] extend K to K′, which includes K as a proper part.   (Chomsky (1993, 1995))

This condition requires that a phrase targeted as the movement operation be extended. It is obvious that the object-raising and the head-raising do not extend VP and v*P, respectively. The same is true of the CP phase of the derivation in (31). As shown in the discussion in Chapter 1, similar operations to those observed in the v*P phase take place in the CP phase: the [uφ] and [NOM] originating in C are inherited by T, which is dominated by CP, and the subject generated in Spec-v* raises to Spec-T.

(35)

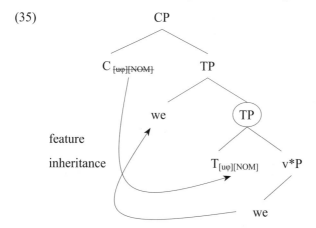

The circled node TP, which is immediately dominated by the CP node, is not extended to the larger projection after the application of the subject raising from Spec-v*.

Given this state of affairs, Tonoike (2008a, b) proposes an "Excorporation Analysis" for English structure-building, as an alternative free from the complications mentioned above.[15]

---

[15] The Excorporation Analysis proposed by Tonoike (2008a, b) is similar to that proposed by Roberts (1991) in that lexical elements form a lexical complex in the course of derivation but different from Roberts' in that, as will be discussed, the Excorporation Analysis allows a lexical element to move with phonetic material of another lexical element.

(36) a. C and T, and v* and V, are drawn from the lexicon as lexical complexes: C-T and v*-V.[16]
b. After v*-V is merged with its complement, v* excorporates and is merged with the VP already built, forming the projection of v*, to which an external argument is merged.
c. After C-T is merged with v*P, forming the projection of T, C excorporates and is merged with TP, projecting C.

Taking (31) as an example, let us examine how the Excorporation Analysis builds its structure. In the v*P phase, v*-V (*build*) is drawn from the lexicon as a lexical complex and merges with the object DP, forming a VP.

(37)

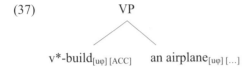

v*-build$_{[u\varphi]\,[ACC]}$ an airplane$_{[u\varphi]\,[...]}$

Contrary to Chomsky (2008) but following Tonoike (2008a, b), we assume that a main verb has unvalued φ-features [uφ] and the case feature [ACC], and that case-assignment (or valuation) is executed under Merge. (Cf. Bošković (2007) and Tonoike (1999))

(38)   In English, case is assigned under Merge to the case-assigning category.

When *v*-build* and its complement *an airplane* are merged, the unvalued case feature [...] of *an airplane* is valued as [ACC] by the main verb *build*, which is a case-assigning category.[17] (Also, (38) has the effect of deriving EPP (Extended Projection Principle) effect to which we will return just below). Although in (37) all the lexical properties that V has are satisfied, those that v* has are not satisfied. Suppose here that v* has a lexical (or selectional) property such that it takes VP as its complement. In order to satisfy this property, v* excorporates from VP and merges with VP to form v*P, to whose specifier the subject *we* is merged.

---

[16] Following Chomsky (2008), we assume that v* and C are phase heads.

[17] We assume that valuation of unvalued φ-features is executed in the same way as in standard Phase Theory, which we went over in Chapter 1.

(39)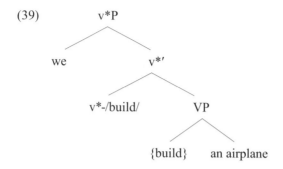

It is worth pointing out here that this analysis is free from the theoretical problems observed above. There are no feature-inheritance operations: contrary to Chomsky (2008), we assume that a main verb inherently carries both [uφ] and [ACC]. There is also no violation of the Extension Condition, instead, V and v* expand cyclically. At this point, we have to mention the head-raising of v*. In (39), v* is raised with the main verb *build*, leaving a copy in the head of the VP. However, our assumption regarding this copy left by the movement operation is crucially different from Chomsky's. Although Chomsky considers the copy still to be a constituent of the moved element, we adopt the Overt Syntax Hypothesis by Tonoike (2008a) and accordingly assume that the Internal Merge (or movement) is always accompanied by phonetic material but leaves its meaning (or semantic features) behind in the original position.

(40) Overt Syntax Hypothesis
Internal Merge must carry an element with a phonetic shape.

In (39), v* undergoes Internal Merge with the phonetic shape of the main verb (*build*), represented as /build/, leaving its meaning, represented as {build}, behind in the original position. We also assume that such formal features as (unvalued) φ-features and case features move along with the phonetic features as a free rider in the sense of Chomsky (1995). This assumption receives support from the fact that the phonetic realization of pronouns depends on their case feature (that is, the distinctions between such pronouns as *he* and *him* are realization of the case features of [NOM] and [ACC], respectively).

It is worth noting here that the violation of the Extension Condition caused by the head-raising of V does not take place in (39): the movement of v* accompanied with /build/ expands the structure from v* to v*′ (or to v*P). In (39), all the lexical properties that v* and V have are satisfied, and thus the complement domain of v* undergoes the Transfer operation.

In the next stage of the derivation, a lexical complex C-T is merged to (39), to form (41). Contrary to Chomsky (2008), we assume that a finite T has inherently unvalued φ-features and the case feature [NOM], and that a declarative C does not have any unvalued features.[18]

(41)

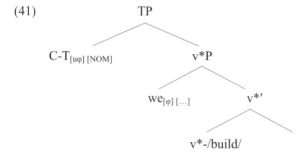

When introduced to the structure (39) above, the subject *we* has valued φ-features and an unvalued case feature [...]. The [uφ] on T serves as a probe and locates the subject, valuing its unvalued φ-features by agreement. The unvalued case feature [...] of the subject also has to be valued. Recall that in English, case is assigned under Merge, as stated in (38). In order for the subject *we* to be assigned case, it has to be merged internally with T carrying the case feature [NOM], as seen in (42) below. Note here that the subject moves along with both its formal features and phonetic features, but leaves its semantic feature behind in the original position.

(42)

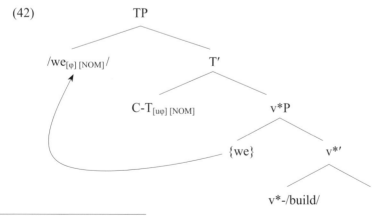

---

[18] Again, this implies that there is no such operation as "feature inheritance."

In the previous analyses, the movement of the subject has been executed in terms of [EPP] of T. As mentioned above, case-assignment in terms of Merge makes it possible to derive the EPP effect. In this context, (38) also gives a principled explanation of why the EPP effect is not observed in simple VPs and PPs: a DP is case-assigned when merged with a V or a P, and hence there is no reason to raise it.

Let us now turn to the derivation of (42), which ceases to proceed at the stage of (42). The null complementizer in (42) does not excorporate and merge to TP because this movement violates the Overt Syntax Hypothesis, given in (40). Neither C nor T in (42) has any phonetic content.[19] The fact that a declarative C does not have uninterpretable (unvalued) features to be checked (valued) is another reason that C does not excorporate: there is no motivation for excorporation, and the subsequent merge violates Last Resort. It is obvious that a declarative C does not have uninterpretable features to be checked, which in turn means it does not have to be excorporated. If C does not move as a part of the lexical complex C-T, it follows that in (41) the structure above the v*P is the projection of both T and C, which implies that the overall structure is at the same time both TP and CP. We will come back to this issue of the dual categorial status of this clause later.

According to the discussion above, C excorporates and merges with TP if C has uninterpretable features to be checked, and phonetic material moves along with it. This can be clearly observed in interrogative sentences.

(43) What did they build?

In (43), C has an interpretable feature [Q] and an uninterpretable feature [uWh], the latter of which is to be checked by an operator that has an interpretable counterpart. Suppose that the derivation of (43) proceeds to (44), where the matrix TP is constructed by merging the lexical complex C-T (*did*).[20, 21]

---

[19] Notice here that even if T contains such an overt modal as *will*, the complex C-*will* does not excorporate and merge to TP, to form CP. We therefore assume that a declarative C does not have any selectional feature that requires it to merge with TP.

[20] We tentatively assume that *do* is generated in T.

[21] The *wh*-phrase *what* moves to the outer Spec-v* in (44).

(44)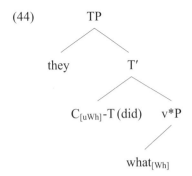

In order for [uWh] of C to be checked, C has to excorporate and merge to TP, forming CP, to whose specifier position a *wh*-operator *what* moves.

(45)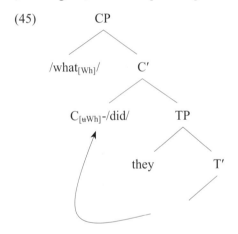

The excorporation of C conforms to the Overt Syntax Hypothesis because it brings phonetic material along with it, namely, the sound of *did* (represented as /*did*/).

In the case of Yes-No interrogatives, we assume with Grimshaw (1993) that an empty operator for Yes-No interrogatives can check [uWh] of C.

(46) a. Did they build an airplane?
b. [CP Op[Wh] [C' C[uWh]-/did/ [TP they [T' ___ [v*P build an airplane]]]]]?

Notice here that the merge of the Yes-No operator Op to Spec-C does not violate the Overt Syntax Hypothesis, because the Op in (46b) is merged not internally but externally: the Overt Syntax Hypothesis applies only to Internal Merge (or Move).

As a final theoretical assumption, we will tentatively adopt the IC, as in (47) below.

(47) The head of an A-chain becomes invisible to further computation when its uninterpretable features are valued. (Chomsky (2008: 150))

We consider that Grammar, at least the grammar of English, cannot dispense with this condition. Consider the following ungrammatical sentences, which show that preposition-stranding does not always give rise to grammatical sentences.

(48) a. *Of which cars* were [the hoods *t*] damaged by the explosion?
 b. **Which cars* were [the hoods of *t*] damaged by the explosion?

Kuno (1973) made an attempt to account for this difference in grammaticality in terms of his Clause Non-Final Incomplete Constituent Constraint, as demonstrated in (49a), together with the notion of Incompleteness, as shown in (49b).

(49) a. Clause Non-Final Incomplete Constituent Constraint
 It is not possible to move any element of a category α in a clause—non-final position out of α if what is left over in α constitutes an incomplete α.
 b. Incompleteness
 An XP α is incomplete if an obligatory element is missing.

Let us first examine the ungrammatical sentence in (48b). The bracketed phrase here is incomplete in that the complement of the preposition *of* is missing and the bracketed phrase is in clause non-final position. In (48a), in contrast, the bracketed phrase is in clause—non-final position, but is not incomplete, because the PP *of which car* is not an obligatory element for N.

It is true that Kuno's Clause Non-Final Incomplete Constituent Constraint can account for the phenomena pointed out in (48), but it remains unclear why (49) holds. The IC, however, seems to give a principled explanation to Kuno's constraint in (49). The *wh*-phrase *which cars* in (48b) is case-assigned when it is merged to the complement of the preposition. Notice that the *wh*-phrase is the head of a trivial A-chain, which means that it is invisible to further computation. Thus, (48b) is ungrammatical. On the other hand, the noun complement *of which car* is not a DP, and thus it does not have to be case-assigned and is movable.

The same phenomena can be observed in *wh*-extraction out of a PP headed by *to*, which is an optional argument of the raising verb *seem*. Observe the following sentences.

(50) a. Tom seems [to Mary] to have caused an accident.
b. [To whom] does Tom seem to have caused an accident?
c. *Who(m) does Tom [to *t*] seem to have caused an accident?

(50a) shows that the complement of the preposition *to* is case-assigned, which means that *Mary* heads a trivial A-chain with its uninterpretable features valued. Thus, as predicted by the IC, although P-stranding *wh*-movement (50c) is impossible, *wh*-movement pied-piping the preposition (50b) is possible.[22]

Although we assume that the IC plays an important role in English grammar, we will argue that in order to rule in grammatical sentences that apparently violate the Subject Condition, the IC should be modified.

In this subsection, we have outlined Tonoike's (2008a, b) Excorporation Analysis and the IC. Armed with these assumptions, we will tackle the difficulty shown in (24), (28), and (30), which the Phase-based approach wrongly excludes as ungrammatical.

2.3.2. An Excorporation Solution

A grammatical sentence that apparently involves a Subject Condition violation is the following.

(51) Of which major is it important for the students to take a course in physics?

As discussed above, the *wh*-phrase *of which major* in (51) is extracted from an infinitival subject introduced with the infinitival complementizer *for*.

To begin with, let us see how the Excorporation Analysis discussed in the previous subsection derives an infinitival clause with a lexical subject introduced by the overt complementizer *for*.

(52) It is important for them to take a course in physics.

---

[22] As is well known, preposition-stranding does not always cause ungrammatical *wh*-movement construction.
(i) Which city do you live in?
In (i) the preposition is stranded but its grammaticality is not degraded. See Egashira and Tonoike (2010) for an explanation of how such extraction is possible under the Excorporation Approach. We will show in Chapter 4 how (i) can be analyzed by the Excorporation Approach.

In the embedded v*P phase, a lexical complex v*-V (*take*) is drawn from the lexicon, merging with the object DP (*a course in physics*) to form a VP, followed by excorporation of v*-/V/ (/*take*/) out of the VP and merge to the VP to from v*', to whose specifier the infinitival subject *them* with [φ] and the unvalued case feature [...] is then merged.[23]

(53)

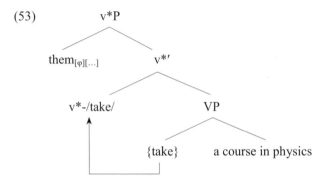

In this v*P phase, all the operations that need to be implemented are completed and the complement domain VP undergoes the Transfer operation. The computation then proceeds to the embedded CP phase. As to the derivation of an infinitival CP introduced with a (lexical) complementizer, we make the following assumptions.

(54) a. In English infinitival clauses with a lexical subject introduced by *for*, a null complementizer C, *for*, and infinitival *to* are drawn from the lexicon as a lexical complex of the form C-*for*-*to*.
 b. This lexical complex excorporates and merges with the structure already built.
 c. The so-called infinitival complementizer *for* belongs to T(ense) and the infinitival *to* to M(odal).[24]

Before we proceed, some comments on the categorial status of infinitival *to* and *for* are in order. Let us begin with infinitival *to*. It has been

---

[23] Regarding feature valuation between the main verb and its object, see the previous discussion in 2.3.1.
[24] Pesetsky and Torrego (2001) propose a similar analysis concerning the categorial status of *for*. They claim that an overt complementizer *that* belongs to T and undergoes head-movement to C. Extending the analysis to infinitival clauses, they further claim that *for* is generated in T and moves to C.
 (i) a. I would prefer for Sue to buy the book.
  b. I would prefer [$_{CP}$ [$_T$for]$_j$ + [C, uT][Sue to$_j$ buy the book]].

widely assumed that infinitival *to* is generated as T. However, as correctly pointed out by Nomura (2006), infinitival *to* behaves in the same way as English modals such as *will, must,* and so on with respect to the form of the verb that follows the modal; that is, an infinitival form of the verb follows infinitival *to* as well as the modals. As argued in Nomura (2006), if a modal auxiliary verb is an independent head with a projection, it is natural to think that infinitival *to* belongs to M(odal) and projects a MP (Modal Phrase). (See Nomura (2006) for details.)

Let us now turn to the embedded CP phase. Following the assumptions in (54), the lexical complex C-[$_T$ *for*]-[$_M$ *to*] merges with the structure in (53).

(55)

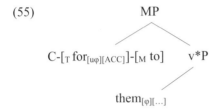

Notice that *for* here inherently has unvalued φ-features and case feature [ACC]. In the next stage of the derivation, the lexical C-[$_T$ *for*$_{[u\varphi][ACC]}$] excorporates and merges with the MP to form the projection of T.

(56)

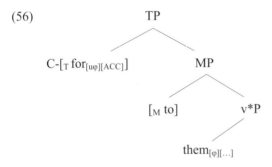

In (56), *for*, which is the head of the TP, serves as a probe and locates the subject in Spec-v*. As a result, agreement holds with respect to φ-features between *for* and the subject. It is worth noticing here that *for* also has case feature [ACC]. Remember that we assume (38), repeated below as (57), for case-assigning in English.

(57) In English case is assigned under Merge to the case-assigning category.

In (56) the case-assigning category is *for*, as T. In order for the infinitival subject *them* in Spec-v* to be assigned the accusative case, it thus has to undergo (Internal) Merge to *for*.

(58)
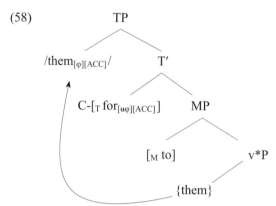

In (58), the unvalued case feature [...] of the subject is valued as [ACC]. In the next stage of the derivation, C excorporates and is merged with TP, forming the projection of C.[25]

(59)
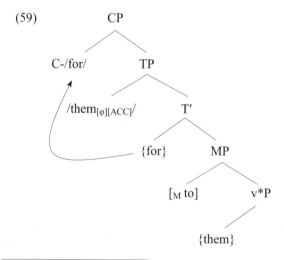

---

[25] It is possible for the derivation to proceed to the matrix clause without projecting a CP. However, such a derivation should be excluded, because the matrix predicate does not select a TP projection.
 (i) *It is not important [$_{TP}$ them [$_{T'}$ C-for [$_{MP}$ to [$_{v*P}$ take a course in physics]]]]
Ungrammaticality in (i) is due to violation of the selectional property of the matrix predicate *important*, not to unwanted word order.

The excorporation of C is executed with a phonetic form of *for*. Given that the reason for this is to derive a correct word order, the excorporation of C with *for* is a kind of "look ahead," which should be avoided. We should remember here that we assume the Overt Syntax Hypothesis, as stated in (40), repeated here as (60).

(60) Overt Syntax Hypothesis
Internal Merge must carry an element with a phonetic shape.

Given (60), the excorporation of C with a phonetic form of *for* follows automatically. (That is, if the excorporation of C were not implemented with it, the derivation would violate (60).) The derived embedded CP is subsequently merged with the rest of the LA to form the whole structure.

(61) [$_{CP/TP}$ It is [$_{vP}$ [$_{AP}$ important [$_{CP}$ for [$_{TP}$ them to [$_{MP}$ [$_{v*P}$ take a course in physics]]]]]]]

One advantage of our analysis of infinitival clauses with a lexical subject introduced by *for* can be found in the system of case-assignment of a lexical subject. It is widely assumed that the configuration of case-assignment of a subject varies depending on the type of clause: nominative case is assigned by finite T, but accusative case is assigned by infinitival C (*for*).

(62)

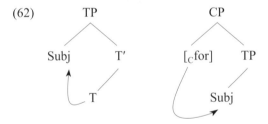

Our analysis based on the assumptions in (54) enables us to unify the mechanisms of case-assignment, because *for*, which has the case feature [ACC], is assumed to be T, and case is assigned under Internal Merge of the subject to T.

(63)

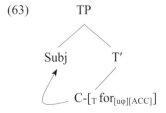

One piece of evidence that lends support to our analysis of infinitival clauses with a lexical subject is obtained from the fact pointed out by Emonds (1985) that no adverbial elements can intervene between *for* and the infinitival subject, as demonstrated in (64) below.

(64) *They intend for *initially* him to be put on probation.

(Emonds (1985: 297))

In the pre-minimalist framework, (64) is excluded by the Case Adjacency Condition: no elements can intervene between a case-assigner and a case-assignee. A theoretical problem with this Case Adjacency Condition, however, is that the case-assignment is defined on the notion of government, which is liable to be dispensed with in the framework of the Minimalist Program.

Matsubara (2002) makes an attempt to exclude ungrammaticality caused by violation of Case Adjacency Condition in terms of the Defective Intervention Effect, introduced by Chomsky (2001) as a locality condition concerning agreement, stating that if probe P matches inactive K that is closer to P than matching M, the agreement relation between P and M is barred.

(65)　　P　　K　　M
　　　　└───×───┘

Matsubara argues that the adverb *initially* is K in (65) that blocks the φ-feature agreement holding between *for* and the infinitival subject *him*. This analysis is made possible by the stipulation that an adverb has inactive φ-features. To the best of my knowledge, no φ-feature agreement relation between DPs and adverbs or between Vs and adverbs has been observed.

(66) *for$_{[\varphi]}$　　initially$_{[\varphi]}$　　him$_{[\varphi]}$
　　　└──────×──────┘

Our Excorporation Analysis, however, can predict the ungrammaticality of (64) in a more natural way. Suppose that the derivation of (64) proceeds to (67), where the lexical complex C-[$_T$ *for*$_{[u\varphi][ACC]}$] excorporates and is merged with MP, forming the projection of T and hosting the lexical subject to its specifier.

(67) [$_{TP}$ /them/ [$_{T'}$ C-[$_T$ for$_{[\varphi][ACC]}$] [$_{MP}$ [$_M$ to] [$_{vP}$ {him} be on probation]]]]

There are two possible derivations: one is excorporation and merge of C-[$_T$ *for*] with TP, as shown in (68a), and the other is merge of the adverb *initially* to TP, as shown in (68b).

(68)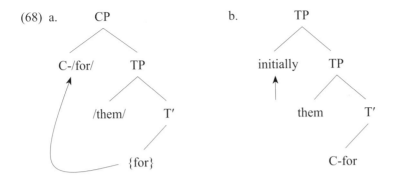

Notice here that the former derivation (i.e., excorporation) followed by the subsequent merge operation is an instance of Internal Merge (IM), while the latter is an instance of External Merge (EM). As demonstrated in 1.2.4, IM is more economical than EM; this means that syntactic computation selects the derivation (68a) rather than (68b), that is, the one derived by IM rather than by EM.[26] We can conclude that the discussion above lends support to the outlined theoretical assumptions for structure-building of infinitival clauses with a lexical subject introduced with *for*.

Now let us go back to (51), repeated below as (69).

(69) Of which major is it important for the students to take a course in physics?

In (69) the *wh*-phrase *of which major* is extracted from the infinitival subject. However, although this extraction is apparently in violation of the Subject Condition, the grammaticality of (69) is not degraded.

In the most deeply embedded v*P phase here, we have (70), where v* excorporates and merges with VP to form v*P, to whose specifier the infinitival subject is merged, and the VP undergoes the Transfer operation.

---

[26] One may argue against the derivation of "IM over EM" on the basis that it wrongly excludes (i) below, because the embedded Spec-T is filled in terms of the EM of an expletive *there* rather than IM of an associate *another war*.

(i) It is possible for there to be another war in the near future.

This difficulty can be overcome if we assume with Deal (2009) that an accusative v projects vP, to whose specifier position an expletive *there* is base-generated.

(ii) [vP there [v' v [VP be [DP another war]]]

In (ii) *there* is selected by v. As to the structure of (ii), see Deal (2009) for details. I owe this point to Heizo Nakajima (p.c.).

(70)　　　　　　　　v*P

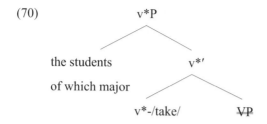

In the embedded CP phase, a lexical complex C-[$_T$ *for*]-[$_M$ *to*] is merged with v*P to form an MP, and the lexical complex C-[$_T$ *for*] subsequently excorporates and merges with the MP to form a TP. *To* need not and hence cannot be pied-piped, because *for* has a phonetic shape and therefore can undergo IM on its own.

(71)　　　　　　　TP

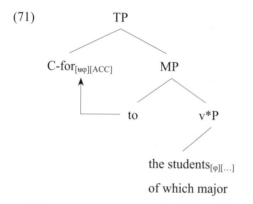

As shown in (71) above, the agreement relation holds between T (*for*) and the infinitival subject with respect to φ-features, as a result of which the unvalued φ-features that *for* has is valued.

In the next stage of the derivation, the infinitival subject is moved to Spec-T for case-theoretic reasons, leaving its semantic features (or meaning) behind.

Chapter 2 On the Subject Condition   49

(72)

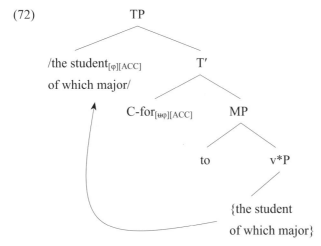

Then, at the final stage of the derivation of the embedded CP phase, the lexical complex C excorporates with /for/ and merges with the TP, forming the projection of C.

(73)

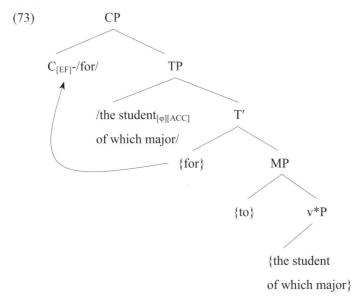

In (73) the infinitival complementizer C-/for/ with [EF] (Edge Feature)

serves as a probe and locates *wh*-phrases.[27] In the case of (73) there are two likely candidates for the [EF] of C to locate: one is a *wh*-phrase in Spec-T and the other in Spec-v*. Attraction of the *wh*-phrase in Spec-v* is impossible, however, because the phrase in Spec-v*, which is a copy, consists only of semantic features, and IM (attraction/movement) of elements with no phonetic shapes is prohibited by the Overt Syntax Hypothesis, as demonstrated in (40), repeated as (74) below.

(74) Overt Syntax Hypothesis
Internal Merge must carry an element with a phonetic shape.

As argued in 2.3.1, a copy of a moved element that is in the original position of that element consists exclusively of sematic features, without any phonetic features. It then follows that extraction of an element from Spec-v* is always impossible.[28]

If the attraction of the *wh*-phrase from Spec-v* is impossible, the remaining option is attraction from Spec-T. However, attraction from Spec-T should be prohibited by the IC: an uninterpretable feature, in this case the unvalued case feature of the infinitival subject, is valued in this position. It then follows that grammatical sentence (69) cannot be derived. However, this difficulty can be overcome by revising the IC along the lines of (75) below, in such a way as to make it possible for a PP to be moved out of a DP in a case position.

(75) Revised Inactivity Condition (RIC)
D and N that head the head of an A-chain become invisible to further computation when its uninterpretable features are valued.

According to (75), D and N are invisible elements, but the rest of DP is not invisible.

(76) [$_{DP}$ D$_{[CASE]}$ [$_{NP}$ N$_{[CASE]}$ PP]]

We indicate invisible elements with shading in (76).

A piece of evidence for the assumption of (75) comes from German. In this language, when a DP is in a case-marked position, case morphology is manifested both in D and in N. Observe German examples (77) below.

---

[27] The [EF] feature of C is omitted from (71) to (72) for ease of exposition. *For* inherently has [EF] in the case of (69).

[28] In our analysis, it is not the Locality Condition but the Overt Syntax Hypothesis that prohibits access to Spec-v*.

(77) a. Der Mann/Student   hat den Lehrer   gesehen.
       the man/student   has the teacher   seen
       'The man/student has seen the teacher.'
    b. Der Lehrer   hat den Mann/Studenten   gesehen.
       the teacher   has the man/student   seen
       'The teacher has seen the man/student.'

(Haegeman (1991: 158))

In (77a), the DP *der Mann/Student* and the DP *den Lehrer* occupy the subject position and the object position, respectively. Conversely, in (77b) the DPs *der Lehrer* and *den Mann/Student* occupy the subject position and the object position, respectively. In each of these sentences, case is morphologically realized on D, with nominative *der* and accusative *den*. What is interesting here is the form of the nouns. Not only D but also the full noun *Student* in German is inflected, depending on the position it occupies.[29] If it is in the subject position, it takes the nominative form *Student*. On the other hand, if it is in the object position it takes the accusative form *Studenten*. These phenomena suggest that D and N in the DP have an unvalued case feature [...], and that they become invisible to further computation when valued.

Another piece of evidence for (75) comes from the fact that *wh*-subextraction is possible from the object of a verb. Observe (78).

(78) Of which driver did you find [a picture *t*]?

In (78) the *wh*-phrase is subextracted from an object position and its grammaticality is not degraded.[30] The DP in the object position is always case-assigned by a transitive verb, but subextraction is always possible. This suggests that elements other than D and N are accessible. Thus, this piece of evidence also lends support to the RIC.

With (75) in mind, let us go back to (73), repeated as (79) below, where irrelevant parts are omitted.

---

[29] Haider (2010) further shows that case is morphologically realized on attributive adjectives in German.

[30] Not only subextraction but also total extraction is possible from a complement of a transitive verb. We will discuss this further in Chapter 4.

(79)

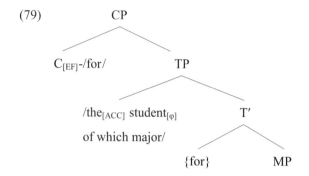

In (79), D (*the*) has a valued case feature and thus is inactive. The infinitival complementizer *for* can locate the *wh*-phrase *of which major* in the subject DP and attract it to its specifier position without incurring a violation of the RIC.[31, 32]

(80)

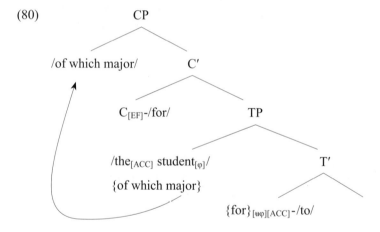

We can successively extract the *wh*-phrase *of which major* to Spec-C, which is available to attraction from an upper phase head: the matrix C.[33] Sup-

---

[31] If a DP is a phase, as argued by Svenonius (2004) and Hiraiwa (2005), *of which car* is raised to Spec-D before being raised out of the subject.

(i) [DP /of which car/ [D′ [D the[ACC]] [NP student {of which major}]]]

[32] Although the RIC states that an unvalued case feature is assigned to both D and N, we assume throughout this book that in English, unlike in German, the unvalued case feature is assigned to D.

[33] Heizo Nakajima (p.c.) points out that the RIC in (75) wrongly generates (i), where an adjunct AP is extracted from the infinitival subject.

pose that the derivation proceeds to the matrix CP as in (81) below. We tentatively assume that the *be*-verb is generated as part of a lexical complex C-T-v-*be*, that this complex undergoes subsequent excorporation and merge operations to form the matrix CP, and that the expletive *it* is generated in Spec-v and then raised to the matrix Spec-T.[34, 35]

(81)

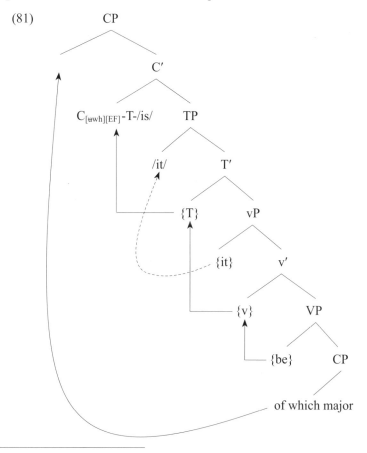

(i) **How afraid of dogs* is it possible for the boy *t* to circumvent the house which keeps many violent dogs?

The ungrammaticality of (i) might be attributed to the fact that the extracted adjunct AP is a reduced relative. I leave this problem for future research.

[34] It is necessary to assume that *be* constitutes a lexical complex with the matrix C and T in order to derive Subject-Auxiliary Inversion. I leave this issue open for future research.

[35] Following Deal (2009), we assume that an expletive is an argument of the main verb and that it is generated in Spec-v.

The matrix C has [uWH] as well as [EF]. C serves as a probe and locates a *wh*-phrase in Spec-C in the embedded clause, thereby attracting it to the matrix-C, where agreement between the *wh*-phrase and [uWH] of C occurs; as a result, an unvalued feature of C is valued.

Before leaving this section, let us turn to (30) in 2.2 above, repeated below as (82), and see how our analysis deals with it.

(82) Of which car is it likely [that the driver ___ caused a scandal][36, 37]

(Kobayashi (2009: 42))

In contrast, in the derivation of infinitival clauses with a lexical subject introduced by *for*, we assume that an embedded declarative complementizer *that* does not form a lexical complex with T.[38] With this assumption in mind, let us now see how (82) is derived. We have (83) below as the derivation of the most deeply embedded v*P phase, where the lexical complex v*-*caused* excorporates and merges with VP to form a v*P to whose specifier the external argument *the driver of which car* is merged.

(83)

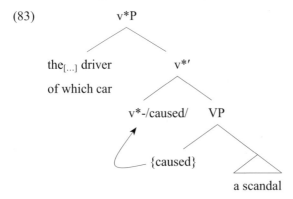

---

[36] I modified (30) slightly by deleting brackets enclosing *that* and *picture*.

[37] It should be noted here that the grammaticality of (82) is not rooted in the grammaticality of its "raising" counterpart.
   (i) Of which car is [the (driver, picture) likely [*t* to [*t* cause a scandal]]]
(Chomsky (2008: 153))
Other predicates than "raising" ones permit subextraction from subjects.
   (ii) a. Of which car do you think that the driver will cause a scandal?
       b. Of which car do you believe that the driver will cause a scandal?
I owe the judgment on (ii) to Eloise Pearson (p.c.).

[38] We will discuss the derivation of an embedded clause without an overt complementizer *that* in the next chapter.

In the next stage of the derivation, T with [uφ] and [NOM] is merged to v*P, and [uφ] is valued under agreement with the subject in Spec-v*. The subject undergoes IM to Spec-T, where the unvalued case feature […] that the subject has is valued as [NOM].

(84)
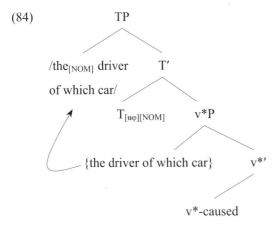

An overt complementizer *that*, which carries [EF], is merged with the TP, forming a CP.

(85)
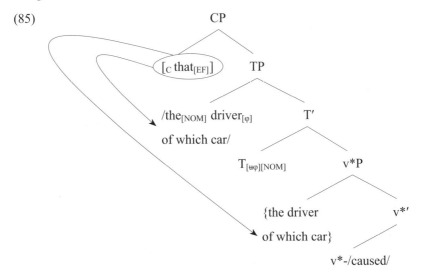

As shown with arrows in (85), *that* with [EF] can serve as a probe and locate two *wh*-phrases: one in Spec-v* and the other in Spec-T.[39] As argued above, the Overt Syntax Hypothesis precludes the *wh*-phrase in Spec-v* from being subextracted, since it does not have any phonetic shapes. Thus, *that* with [EF] attracts a *wh*-phase to Spec-C from Spec-T. Worthy of notice, RIC allows *wh*-subextraction to be implemented from the case-assigned position because elements other than D are active and hence accessible. Thus, our theory can derive (82) correctly, while the phase-based theory wrongly excludes it.

Finally, we should clarify the reason why the overt complementizer *that* does not form a lexical complex with T. We have argued that the infinitival null complementizer C forms a lexical complex with *for*, whose categorial status is T, and that this assumption enables us to exclude an ungrammatical sentence with an adverb intervening between *for* and the infinitival subject in terms of economy.

(86) a. *They intend for initially him to be put on probation.
 b. [TP him [T' C-for to be put on probation]]
 c. *initially* [TP him [T' C-for to be put on probation]]

The IM of C-*for* demonstrated in (86b) is more economical than the EM of *initially* in (86c). Thus, the computation selects (86b).

Contrary to the infinitival clause given in (86), however, an adverb can intervene between an overt complementizer *that* and a subject, as shown in (87).

(87) They intend that *initially* he should be put on probation.

(Emonds (1985: 297))

The grammaticality of (87) suggests that an overt complementizer *that* does not form a lexical complex with T; otherwise, (87) would be excluded in the same way as (86) is.

Furthermore, as will be argued in the next chapter, this analysis enables us to explain the *that*-trace effect in a natural way.

---

[39] We implicitly assume that *wh*-agreement holds between that *that* and the *wh*-phrase in Spec-T.

2.3.3. Subextraction from Matrix Clause Subjects

In the previous section, we saw how our Excorporation Analysis, together with the RIC, could explain the grammaticality of sentences where *wh*-extraction takes place from the subject, as seen in (88) below.

(88) a. Of which major is it important for the students *t* to take a course in physics?
 b. Of which car is it likely that the driver *t* caused a scandal?

Our next task is to examine whether or not our analysis can also correctly exclude such run-of-the-mill examples of Subject Condition violation as those in Chomsky (2008) and Huang (1982). The sentence to be analyzed here is the following, where subextraction of a *wh*-phrase takes place from a subject of a matrix clause.

(89) *Of which car did the driver *t* cause a scandal?

Our analysis appears to rule wrongly in (89), because the RIC allows rather free subextraction of a *wh*-phrase from a case-assigned position. In order to see this, let us examine the derivation of (89). Suppose that this derivation proceeds through to (90), where the matrix v*P is constructed through excorporation and merge of v*-*caused* and the subject is merged with the projection of v*.

(90)

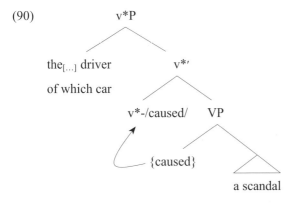

In the next stage of the derivation, a lexical complex C-T(*did*) is merged to (90), thereby forming the projection of T. Notice here that T has [uφ] and case feature [NOM] and that the v*P internal subject is attracted to Spec-T for case-theoretic reasons.

(91)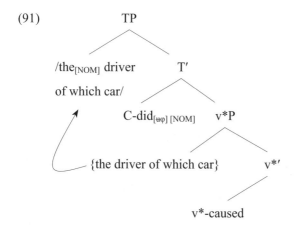

In (91), the unvalued case feature of the subject [...] is valued as [NOM] in Spec-T. In the next stage of the derivation, the lexical complex $C_{[EF]}$-/*did*/ excorporates and merges with TP.

(92)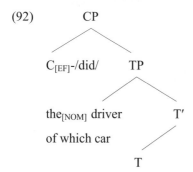

Our analysis predicts that C with [EF] will serve as a probe, locate the *wh*-phrase *of which car*, and attract it to Spec-C, because RIC does allow this kind of extraction to be implemented, due to the fact that it is D (*the*) but not PP (*of which car*) that is case-assigned, which should not be the case, as indicated by the ungrammaticality of (89).

However, there is also the possibility that other principles of grammar will exclude this kind of sentence. There is a grammatical counterpart to (89); observe (93).

(93)   The driver of which car caused a scandal?[40]

---

[40] I owe Eloise Pearson (p.c.) for this grammatical judgment.

In contrast with (89), (93) lacks Subject-Aux Inversion (or *do*-support) and also extraction of *wh*-phrase *of which car*. If we can successfully derive (93) rather than (89), we can maintain our Excorporation Analysis of *wh*-extraction from the subject of an embedded clause, together with the RIC. In what follows, we will explore this line of analysis.

Before going on to the analysis of (89) and (93), however, we will introduce some theoretical assumptions made by Tonoike (2000) concerning features for *wh*-movement. Tonoike argues that a *wh*-phrase should have a focus feature [F] as well as a [wh] feature; the former has a property of taking scope, which triggers *wh*-movement (in Tonoike's terms, Focus movement), while the latter functions to identify a *wh*-word. Tonoike further claims that [wh] must be contained in an [F] constituent. This assumption can account for the following examples, where a larger DP containing a *wh*-phrase undergoes Focus movement to Spec-C, as in (94b, c) and where a *wh*-phrase itself undergoes Focus Movement, as in (94a).[41]

(94) a. ***Which reports*** does the government prescribe the colors of the covers of *t*?
    b. ***The covers of which reports*** does the government prescribe the colors of *t*?
    c. ***The colors of the covers of which reports*** does the government prescribe *t*?   (Tonoike (2000: 217))

The DP in (94), which is a complement of the verb *prescribe*, schematically has the following structure.

(95) a. [$_{DP1}$ the colors of [$_{DP2}$ the covers of [$_{DP3}$ [F] which reports]]]
    b. [$_{DP1}$ the colors of [$_{DP2}$ [F] the covers of [$_{DP3}$ which reports]]]
    c. [$_{DP1}$ [F] the colors of [$_{DP2}$ the covers of [$_{DP3}$ which reports]]]

The focus feature [F] is optionally assigned to a DP. As (95) demonstrates,

---

[41] The examples in (94) are based on Ross (1967), who showed that a larger DP can undergo Relativization.
  (i) a. the report ***which*** the government prescribes the height of the lettering on the covers of *t*.
    b. the report ***the covers of which*** the government prescribes the height of the lettering on *t*.
    c. the report ***the lettering on the covers of which*** the government prescribe the height of *t*.
    d. the report ***the height of the lettering on the covers of which*** the government prescribes *t*.   (Ross (1967: 11–12))

an interpretable focus feature [F] is assigned to each DP. Now, let us observe how (94) is derived, transplanting the assumption concerning [F] into the current framework. We assume that a focus feature [F] is assigned to a phase head, (i.e., C or v*) as well as a DP which undergoes *wh*-movement, and further that [F] assigned to a phase head is uninterpretable—indicated as [uF]—on the one hand, while [F] assigned to DP is interpretable, on the other. Thus, in the v*P phase of (94) we have (96), where v*P is constructed by excorporation and subsequent merge of v*$_{[uF]}$-/*prescribe*/, and merge of external argument *the government*.

(96)

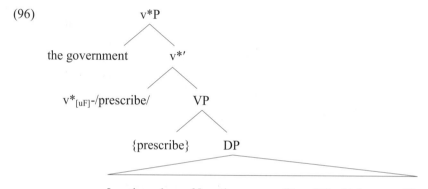

a. [$_{DP1}$ the colors of [$_{DP2}$ the covers of [$_{DP3}$ [F] which reports]]]
b. [$_{DP1}$ the colors of [$_{DP2}$ [F] the covers of [$_{DP3}$ which reports]]]
c. [$_{DP1}$ [F] the colors of [$_{DP2}$ the covers of [$_{DP3}$ which reports]]]

The uninterpretable focus feature [uF] of v* must be checked and deleted; otherwise, the derivation will crash in the v*P phase. Depending on which DP contains an interpretable counterpart for v* with [uF], the following three types of derivation are derived: DP3 in (97a), DP2 in (97b), and DP1 in (97c) undergo IM to the outer spec-v*.

(97) a. [$_{v*P}$ [$_{DP3}$ [F] /which reports/] [$_{v*'}$ the government [$_{v*'}$ v*-/prescribe/ [$_{VP}$ {prescribe} the colors of the covers of {$_{DP3}$ which reports}]]]]
b. [$_{v*P}$ [$_{DP2}$ [F] /the covers of which reports/] [$_{v*'}$ the government [$_{v*'}$ v*-/prescribe/ [$_{VP}$ {prescribe} the colors of {$_{DP2}$ the covers of which reports}]]]]
c. [$_{v*P}$ [$_{DP1}$ [F] /the colors of the covers of which reports/] [$_{v*'}$ the government [$_{v*'}$ v*-/prescribe/ [$_{VP}$ {prescribe} {$_{DP1}$ the colors of the covers of which reports}]]]]

In the next stage of the derivation, in (97), the lexical complex C-T (*does*) merges with v*Ps', followed by the IM of the external argument to TP.[42]

(98) a. [$_{TP}$ /the government/ C$_{[uF]}$-does [$_{v*P}$ [$_{DP3}$ [F] /which reports/] [$_{v*'}$ {the government} [$_{v*}$ v*-/prescribe/ [$_{VP}$ {prescribe} the colors of the covers of {$_{DP3}$ which reports}]]]]]

b. [$_{TP}$ /the government/ C$_{[uF]}$-does [$_{v*P}$ [$_{DP2}$ [F] /the covers of which reports/] [$_{v*'}$ {the government} [$_{v*}$ v*-/prescribe/ [$_{VP}$ {prescribe} the colors of {$_{DP2}$ the covers of which reports}]]]]]

c. [$_{TP}$ /the government/ C$_{[uF]}$-does [$_{v*P}$ [$_{DP1}$ [F] /the colors of the covers of which reports/] [$_{v*'}$ {the government} [$_{v*}$ v*-/prescribe/ [$_{VP}$ {prescribe} {$_{DP1}$ the colors of the covers of which reports}]]]]]

In (98), the external argument *the government* is assigned the nominative case by T (*does*). Notice here that the C part of the lexical complex C-T has an uninterpretable feature [uF]; in order for this feature to be checked and deleted, C must undergo excorporation and subsequent merge with TP, forming a projection of C, in order to host an appropriate *wh*-phrase.[43]

(99) a. [$_{CP}$ C$_{[uF]}$-/does/ [$_{TP}$ /the government/ {does} [$_{v*P}$ [$_{DP3}$ [F] /which reports/] [$_{v*'}$ {the government} [$_{v*}$ v*-/prescribe/ [$_{VP}$ {prescribe} the colors of the covers of {$_{DP3}$ which reports}]]]]]]

b. [$_{CP}$ C$_{[uF]}$-/does/ [$_{TP}$ /the government/ {does} [$_{v*P}$ [$_{DP2}$ [F] /the covers of which reports/] [$_{v*'}$ {the government} [$_{v*}$ v*-/prescribe/ [$_{VP}$ {prescribe} the colors of {$_{DP2}$ the covers of which reports}]]]]]]

c. [$_{CP}$ C$_{[uF]}$-/does/ [$_{TP}$ /the government/ does [$_{v*P}$ [$_{DP1}$ [F] /the colors of the covers of which reports/] [$_{v*'}$ {the government} [$_{v*}$ v*-/prescribe/ [$_{VP}$ {prescribe} {$_{DP1}$ the colors of the covers of which reports}]]]]]]

In (100) below, the uninterpretable [uF] is checked by the interpretable counterpart of the moved DP, and deleted as a result.

---

[42] We tentatively assume that *do* is generated in T.
[43] Assuming multiple specifiers, it is possible to check C's [uF] in the projection of TP.
   (i) *[$_{TP}$ [$_{DP3}$ [F] /which reports/$_i$ [$_{TP}$ /the government/ C$_{[uF]}$-does [$_{v*P}$ t_i [$_{v*'}$ v*-/prescribe/ [$_{VP}$ the colors of the covers of {$_{DP3}$ which reports}]]]]]
Given the requirement that a *wh*-phrase be in a scope position, that is, in Spec-C, (i) can be excluded in a natural way.

(100) a. [CP [DP3 [F] /which reports/] [C' C[uF]-/does/ [TP /the government/ {does} [v*P {DP3 [F] which reports} [v*' {the government} [v*' v*-/prescribe/ [VP {prescribe} the colors of the covers of {DP3 which reports}]]]]]]]

b. [CP [DP2 [F] /the covers of which reports/] [C' C[uF]-/does/ [TP /the government/ {does} [v*P {DP2 [F] the covers of which reports} [v*' {the government} [v*' v*-/prescribe/ [VP {prescribe} the colors of {DP2 the covers of which reports}]]]]]]]

c. [CP [DP1 [F] /the colors of the covers of which reports/] [C' C[uF]-/does/ [TP /the government/ does [v*P /DP1 [F] the colors of the covers of which reports/ [v*' {the government} [v*' v*-/prescribe/ [VP {prescribe} {DP1 the colors of the covers of which reports}]]]]]]]

We have examined Tonoike's (2000) proposal that *wh*-movement is driven by a focus feature [F] and observed that the analysis can correctly derive *wh*-interrogatives in which a larger DP containing a *wh*-phrase is fronted. With this analysis in mind, let us now turn to (93) and (89), both repeated here as (101).

(101) a. The driver of which car caused a scandal? (=(93))
b. *Of which car did the driver cause a scandal? (=(89))

In the v*P phase of (101), the projection of v* is constructed by excorporation and subsequent merge of v*-/cause/. We assume that v* has an uninterpretable [F] feature, and a θ-feature that must be discharged onto the external argument.[44]

(102)

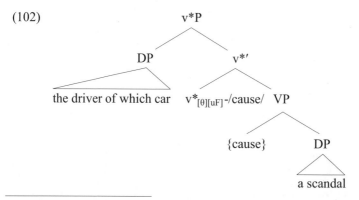

---

[44] We implicitly assume that V and P also have a θ-feature that triggers merge of an argument.

In (102), the θ-feature of v* triggers merge of the external argument *the driver of which car*, as a result of which the θ-role of agent is discharged onto the subject DP. Notice here that the [uF] that v* has must be checked and deleted in this stage of the derivation, which otherwise would crash the derivation in the v*P phase. If there is an element that has interpretable [F] in the search space of v*, it is raised to outer Spec-v*, as we have seen in the derivation presented from (96) to (100). In (102), there are no such elements in the c-command domain of v*; the candidate that can check and delete uninterpretable [uF] is the subject. At this point, we need to examine the structure of the subject DP. The following is one conceivable structure.

(103) [DP the driver [PP of [DP which car]]]

Assuming along with Tonoike (2000) that an interpretable [F] feature is assigned to a specifier position, there are three such specifier positions in (103); namely, a Spec-D that is deeply embedded, Spec-P, and another Spec-D that is topmost.

(104) a. [DP the driver [PP of [DP [F] which car]]]
b. [DP the driver [PP [F] of [DP which car]]]
c. [DP [F] the driver [PP of [DP which car]]]

Given that an interpretable [F] percolates up to its maximal projection, in (104) the most deeply embedded DP, the PP, and the topmost DP each take on a focus property. If so, the last option, assigning interpretable [F] to topmost Spec-D, makes it possible for uninterpretable [F] of v* to be checked and deleted, because as shown in (105), the DP that has [F] and the v* that has [uF] are in a Spec-head configuration.[45]

(105)

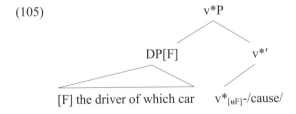

We have observed that an [uF] of v* enters a checking relation when a sub-

---

[45] We assume that in interrogative sentences, v* as well as C in matrix clauses obligatory have an uninterpretable focus feature [uF] on one hand, while v* in embedded clause does not have [uF] on the other. This assumption allows PP-extraction from embedded clauses but prohibits it from matrix clauses.

ject is merged for θ-theoretic reasons, and that iff an interpretable [F] is assigned to the topmost Spec-D, the convergent derivation can be derived.

Now, let us proceed to the CP phase. Here, a lexical complex C-T is merged with v*P. As argued above, T has case feature [NOM] and (topmost) D of the subject DP has an unvalued case feature [...]. The subject DP is raised to Spec-T for case-theoretic reasons.

(106)

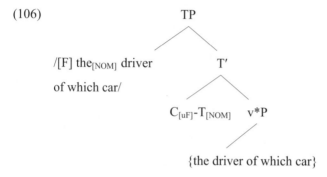

In the configuration of (106), uninterpretable features related to T are checked. The remaining unchecked feature is the [uF] of C. One possible derivation that could check and delete this feature would involve excorporating the lexical complex C-T and merging it with TP, projecting a CP for the landing site of a *wh*-phrase. However, this excorporation cannot be executed, because neither T nor C has a phonetic form. The movement of a phonetically empty category violates the Overt Syntax Hypothesis, which is repeated below as (107).

(107) Overt Syntax Hypothesis
 Internal Merge must carry an element with a phonetic shape.

The uninterpretable [F] of C can be checked by the subject DP, whose maximal projection has [F], because the subject is in the checking domain of the C-T complex. One may argue, against our analysis, that the *wh*-phrase is not in the scope position, that is, not in Spec-C. However, remember here the discussion in 2.3.1, in which we show that the projection of the C-T complex can form a dual-categorial projection if C and T are phonetically empty and do not have uninterpretable features, as is the case in (108).[46] It then follows that not only the TP but also the CP in (108) is the projection

---

[46] Remember that the [uF] of C and the [NOM] of T are checked as a result of entering a checking relation.

right above v*P.

(108)

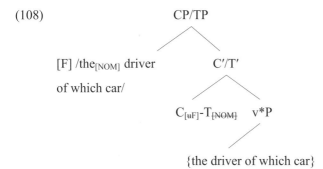

We conclude that our analysis can correctly derive (101a).

Before leaving this section, we have to touch upon the ungrammaticality of (101b). In order to explain the ungrammaticality of (101b), it is useful to examine the following sentences containing a modal auxiliary verb *will*.

(109) a. The driver of which car will cause a scandal?
b. *Of which car will the driver cause a scandal?

The derivation in the v*P phase in (109) is the same as that in (101a). When a subject is merged with the v* projection for θ-theoretic reasons, the subject DP with its interpretable [F] enters into a checking relation with the [uF] of v*. As a result, the uninterpretable [uF] of v* is checked and deleted.

(110) [$_{v*P}$ [$_{DP}$ [F] the driver of which car] [$_{v*'}$ v*$_{[uF]}$-/cause/]]

In the CP phase of (110), we assume that a Modal constitutes a lexical complex with C-T and that the lexical complex C-T-*will* is merged with v*P, projecting an MP.

(111) [$_{MP}$ C-T-will [$_{v*P}$ [$_{DP}$ [F] the driver of which car] [$_{v*'}$ v*$_{[uF]}$-/cause/]]]

In the next stage of the derivation, C-T-/*will*/ excorporates and merges with the MP. It is worth noticing here that C has an uninterpretable focus feature [uF], T has a case feature [NOM], and the D of the subject DP has an unvalued case feature [...] and an uninterpretable [F] is assigned to Spec-D.

(112) [$_{TP}$ C$_{[uF]}$-T$_{[NOM]}$-/will/ [$_{MP}${will} [$_{v*P}$ [$_{DP}$ [F] the$_{[...]}$ driver of which car] [$_{v*'}$ v*$_{[uF]}$-/cause/]]]]

The subject DP generated in Spec-v* is searched for and located by T, which has a case feature [NOM]; as a result, the subject DP undergoes Internal Merge to Spec-T. Remember the discussion above, where we claimed that uninterpretable [uF] can be checked by a DP that has interpretable [F]; the same analysis can be applied here. Just as in a v*P phase, uninterpretable [uF] of v* is checked when the subject is merged for θ-theoretic reasons, the uninterpretable [uF] of C enters a checking relation with the subject when raised for case-theoretic reasons.

(113) [$_{CP/TP}$ [$_{DP}$ [F] /the$_{[NOM]}$ driver of which car/] [$_{C'/T'}$ C$_{[uF]}$-T$_{[NOM]}$-/will/ [$_{MP}$ {will} [$_{v*P}$ {the driver of which car} [$_{v*'}$ v*$_{[uF]}$-/cause/]]]]]

At the stage of the derivation in (113), all uninterpretable features are checked and deleted, and the *wh*-phrase is in the scope position, Spec-C, because of the dual categorial status of the topmost projection; this means that the derivation is completed.

It might be objected, against our analysis, that the lexical complex C-T can excorporate and merge to the projection of T, delaying checking of the [uF] of C, because this excorporation and merge of the lexical complex is accompanied by a phonetic shape /*will*/, and might be claimed on this basis that it should be possible to derive (109b).

(114) a. [$_{CP}$ C$_{[uF]}$-T$_{[NOM]}$-/will/ [$_{TP}$ [$_{DP}$ [F] /the$_{[NOM]}$ driver of which car/] [$_{T'}$ [$_{MP}$ {will} [$_{v*P}$ {the driver of which car} [$_{v*'}$ v*$_{[uF]}$-/cause/]]]]]]
 b. [$_{CP}$ /of which car/ [$_{C'}$ C$_{[uF]}$-T$_{[NOM]}$-/will/ [$_{TP}$ [$_{DP}$ [F] /the$_{[NOM]}$ driver {of which car}/] [$_{T'}$ [$_{MP}$ {will} [$_{v*P}$ z{the driver of which car} [$_{v*'}$ v*$_{[uF]}$-/cause/]]]]]]]

However, this derivation is impossible in our analysis because the Spec-P does not have an interpretable [F], which, in turn, means that the [uF] of C cannot be checked and deleted. A potential alternative step toward convergent derivation would be to move the whole subject DP, to whose topmost Spec-D an interpretable [F] is assigned.

(115) [$_{CP}$ [$_{DP}$ [F] /the driver of which car/] [$_{C'}$ C$_{[uF]}$-T$_{[NOM]}$-/will/ [$_{TP}$ {$_{DP}$ [F] the$_{[NOM]}$ driver of which car}] [$_{T}$ [$_{MP}$ {will} [$_{v*P}$ [$_{v*'}$ v*$_{[uF]}$-/cause/]]]]]]]

However, this derivation is excluded by that of (113) on grounds of derivational economy (the derivation of (113) involves fewer operations than that of (115)).

Similar consideration holds for ungrammatical sentence (101b), repeated below as (116).

(116) *Of which car did the driver cause a scandal? (=(89), (101b))

Suppose that this derivation proceeds to the final stage of the v*P phase, in which the topmost Spec-D has interpretable [F], which checks and deletes the uninterpretable [uF] that v* has when the subject is merged to the v* projection for θ-theoretic reasons.

(117) [$_{v*P}$ [$_{DP}$ [F] the driver of which car] [$_{v*'}$ v*$_{[uF]}$-/cause/]]]

Assuming that the dummy *do* belongs to the Modal, the lexical complex C-T-*did* is merged to v*P at an early stage of the derivation of CP phase, forming an MP.

(118) [$_{MP}$ C-T-did [$_{v*P}$ [$_{DP}$ [F] the $_{[...]}$ driver of which car] [$_{v*'}$ v*$_{[uF]}$-/cause/]]]

Here, C and T have an uninterpretable focus feature [uF] and a case feature [NOM], respectively; the D of the subject DP also has an unvalued case feature [...]. In the next stage of the derivation, C-T-/*did*/ excorporates and merges with MP, forming TP, and the subject is raised to Spec-T for case-theoretic reasons.

(119) [$_{CP/TP}$ [$_{DP}$ [F] the$_{[NOM]}$ driver of which car] [$_{C/T'}$ C$_{[uF]}$-T$_{[NOM]}$-/did/ [$_{MP}$ {did} [$_{v*P}$ {the driver of which car} [$_{v*'}$ v*$_{[uF]}$-/cause/]]]]]

In (119), it is possible for a subject DP with an interpretable focus feature [F] to enter a checking relation with a C that has an uninterpretable focus feature [uF]. As a result, all uninterpretable features will be checked and deleted. In this case, the topmost projection has dual categorial status, both TP and CP, and the *wh*-interrogative takes scope in CP.

It would be possible to excorporate C$_{[uF]}$-T-*did* and merge it with the TP, forming the projection of C, with which the *wh*-phrase *of which car* is merged.

(120) [$_{CP}$ /of which car/ [$_{C'}$ C$_{[uF]}$-T$_{[NOM]}$-/did/ [$_{TP}$[$_{DP}$ [F] the$_{[NOM]}$ driver {of which car}] [$_{T'}$ [$_{MP}$ {did} [$_{v*P}$ {the driver of which car} [$_{v*'}$ v*$_{[uF]}$-/cause/]]]]]]

As argued above, in the configuration of (120) it is impossible to check and delete [uF] of C because the PP *of which car* does not have an interpretable focus feature [F]. Thus, (116) is ungrammatical. Rather, (121) is a convergent derivation, in which the whole subject *the driver of which car* is merged with the CP, and an interpretable focus feature [F] of the subject checks and deletes the [uF] of C.

(121) [$_{CP/TP}$ [/[F] the driver of which car/] [$_{C/T'}$ C$_{[uF]}$-T$_{[NOM]}$-/did/ [$_{TP}$ [$_{DP}$ {the driver of which car}] [$_{T'}$ [$_{MP}$ {did}[$_{v*P}$ {the driver of which car} [$_{v*'}$ v*$_{[uF]}$-/cause/]]]]]]]

However, (121) is excluded by (119), again on grounds of derivational economy ((119) contains fewer operations than (121)).[47]

To conclude, before moving to the next chapter, we should reconsider the derivation of the two sentences that much of the discussion in the present chapter centers on, in particular with respect to the [F] feature, which drives *wh*-movement.

(122) a. Of which major is it important for the students to take a course in physics?
  b. Of which car is it likely that the driver caused the accident?

It can be considered that the subjects of the embedded clauses here have the following structures, and that an interpretable [F] feature is assigned to the Spec-P.

(123) a. [$_{DP}$ the students [$_{PP}$ [F] of which major]]
  b. [$_{DP}$ the driver [$_{PP}$ [F] of which car]]

We do not assume that all phase heads are assigned the uninterpretable [uF], but only that matrix phase heads of interrogative sentences are assigned [uF].[48] Thus, in (122), the C of the matrix interrogative clause is assigned [uF], which attracts a focused phrase in Spec-C of the embedded CP.

(124) a. [$_{CP}$ of which major [$_{C'}$ C$_{[uF]}$-is [$_{TP}$ it .... [$_{CP}$ of which major [$_{C'}$ C$_{[uF]}$-for
  b. [$_{CP}$ of which major [$_{C'}$ C$_{[uF]}$-is [$_{TP}$ it .... [$_{CP}$ of which car [$_{C'}$ that$_{[uF]}$

When [F] is assigned to the topmost Spec-D in (123), the overall DP

---

[47] As is well known, when a subject is a *wh*-interrogative, *do* is absent. There seem to be several ways to achieve this. One is to assume that when a topmost Spec-D has [F] and the subject DP contains a *wh*-phrase, "M (*do*)" part of the lexical complex C-T-*do*, is deleted in the Lexical Array when drawn from the Lexicon, and computation goes on as shown in the derivation of (101).

Another way is to assume that in the overt syntax, the computation utilizes C-T-*do*, as shown in the derivation in (119). Adopting the assumption by Radford (2009) that Affix-Hopping applies in the PF component, *do* is deleted when a subject has [F] and contains a [wh] feature. I leave this issue open for future research.

[48] See footnote 45 for the assignment of [uF].

is extracted. This is "total *wh*-extraction," which we will discuss further in Chapter 3.

(125) a. *[DP [F] Who] is it important for to take a course in physics?
b. *[DP [F] Who] is it likely that caused an accident?

Chapter 3

Total Extraction

This chapter explores various consequences of our analysis proposed in Chapter 2. In that chapter, we demonstrated how Excorporation Analysis, together with the RIC (Revised Inactivity Condition), derives constructions involving *wh*-subextraction from a subject.

(1) a. Of which major is it important for the students to take a course in physics?
　　b. Of which car is it likely that the driver caused the accident?

In (1a) and (1b), a *wh*-phrase is subextracted from the subject of the embedded clause, in violation of the Subject Condition. However, as shown by the grammaticality of (1), no violation is incurred. We have observed in the previous chapter that our analysis can correctly predict the grammaticality of (1).

What we have to do next is turn our attention to total extraction from subjects. It is well known that the total extraction of a *wh*-phrase from a subject gives rise to ungrammaticality.

(2) a. *Who is it important for t to take a course in physics?
　　b. *Who is it likely that t caused the accident?

The sentences in (2) show the so-called "overt C(omp) trace effect" (in the narrow sense, (2a) has a "*for*-trace effect" and (2b) has a "*that*-trace effect"). More accurately, in our present terms, we are observing "Overt C-copy effects." These effects are obviated when an overt C is deleted.

(3) a. Who do you prefer to go?[1]
　　b. Who is it likely caused the accident?

This chapter will show that our analysis accounts for overt C-copy effects in a more natural way than other analyses, including pre-Minimalist analyses. As a starting point, we will show how these phenomena were analyzed in pre-Minimalism, in 3.1. In the next section, 3.2, it will be shown that our analysis can account for these phenomena more simply and elegantly than the pre-Minimalist analysis. In 3.3, our analysis will be compared to the analysis of Rizzi and Shlonsky (2007).

3.1. Pre-Minimalist Approach

In this section we will give a brief overview Chomsky's (1986a) and Rizzi's (1990) approaches, which are similar in that they both make an attempt to attribute the ungrammaticality of overt C-trace effects to the ECP (Empty Category Principle); however, they differ in their treatment of complementizers.

3.1.1. Chomsky's (1986a) Approach: Rigid Minimality[2]

Chomsky analyzes *that*-trace phenomena, as exemplified in (4), in terms of the ECP.

(4) a. who did you believe [$_{CP}$ t′ [$_{C'}$ e [$_{IP}$ t would win]]]
　　b. *who did you believe [$_{CP}$ t′ [$_{C'}$ that [$_{IP}$ t would win]]]

(Chomsky (1986a: 47))

The ECP, which is defined in (5) below, is based on the notion of "government."

(5) a. ECP: A trace must be properly governed.
　　b. Proper Government: α properly governs β iff α governs β and
　　　(i) α is N, V, or A or
　　　(ii) α is co-indexed with β

---

[1] An ungrammatical counterpart of (3a) is as follows.
　(i) *Who do you prefer for *t* to go?
Needless to say, (2a) cannot be saved even though *for* is deleted.

[2] "Rigid" is the term coined by Rizzi (1990), who contrasts it with his "Relativized" Minimality.

Chomsky also uses the notion of Minimality, which is a subtype of barrier.

(6) ...α...[$_{\gamma'}$ ...γ^0...β...]

In the configuration of (6), if γ is a zero-level category and γ' is a bar-level category in the sense of X-bar theory, γ' constitutes Minimality for government of α, a subtype of barrier.[3] ECP, coupled with Minimality, excludes (4b) as ungrammatical in the following way. In (4b), the original trace in Spec-I (=T) is an offending trace because it is protected from government by the V (*believe*), whereas C' constitutes a case of Minimality due to the presence of C^0 (*that*). Notice that the overt C (*that*) by definition cannot serve as a governor, nor is the trace in Spec-I (T) antecedent-governed by the intermediate trace in Spec-C, due to the presence of C', which again constitutes Minimality.

Let us now turn to (4a), which is grammatical. Here, the complementizer is not overt, but covert. Chomsky (1986a) claims that a covert C does not have any features (it is "featureless," in his term), and that a featureless X^0 category does not project an intermediate projection X'. According to this analysis, there is no γ' in (6), as a result of which there are no barriers to β's being governed by α. In (4a), C', which would constitute Minimality, does not exist at all because of the featureless C, and so V (*believe*) governs the original trace in Spec-I (T), while the intermediate trace in Spec-C also antecedent-governs the trace in Spec-I (T). Thus, (4a) is grammatical.

Although Chomsky does not extend his analysis of *that*-trace effect to the *for*-trace effect, it is possible to do so. Let us briefly examine how his ECP, together with the notion of Minimality, handles the *for*-trace effect.[4]

(7) a. Who do you prefer [t$_{who}$ C [t$_{who}$ to win]]?
    b. *Who do you prefer [$_{CP}$ t'$_{who}$ [$_{C'}$ for [t$_{who}$ to win]]?[5]

(Rizzi and Shlonsky (2007: 147))

Let us examine (7b) first. The presence of an overt C (*for*) here makes it possible for the intermediate projection of C (C') to constitute Minimality by definition. This C' bans the original trace in Spec-I (T) from being governed by the V (*prefer*); it also prevents the original trace in Spec-I (T) from being

---

[3] Minimality is a special case of a "barrier" for government, in that an X-bar level category constitutes a barrier. Only a maximal projection constitutes a barrier.

[4] Before the era of Government and Binding Theory, Chomsky and Lasnik (1977) derived the *for*-trace effect in terms of a *[for-to] filter.

[5] In (7b), CP ([$_{CP}$] and the intermediate trace in Spec-C (t'$_{who}$) are added to the original example cited from Rizzi and Shlonsky (2007: 147).

antecedent-governed by the intermediate trace in Spec-C (t'_{who}). Thus, (7b) is ungrammatical.

We now turn to (7a). Here, the embedded C is not overt but covert. This means that C in (7a) is featureless, and further that a featureless X^0 category does not project an intermediate projection and thus constitutes Minimality. It then follows that in (7a) no barriers exist preventing government of the original trace by the V (*prefer*), and that the intermediate trace in Spec-C antecedent-governs the original trace in Spec-I.

3.1.2. Rizzi's (1990) Approach: Relativized Minimality

Rizzi (1990) also made an attempt to explain *that*-trace effects using his own ECP, which is presented in (8) below.

(8) ECP: A nonpronominal empty category must be
    (i) properly head-governed (Formal licensing)
    (ii) Theta-governed or antecedent-governed (Identification)
(Rizzi (1990: 32))

The definitions of "head-government," "theta-government," and "antecedent-government" that apply here, and that of "Relativized Minimality," are as follows.

(9) Head-government: X head-governs Y iff
    (i) a. X is a head
        b. X m-commands Y
    (ii) X={[±V ±N], Agr, T}
    (iii) a. no barrier intervenes
        b. Relativized Minimality is respected   (Ibid.: 1990: 25)

(10) Theta-government
    α θ-governs β iff α is a zero-level category that θ-marks β, and α, β are sisters, or β is the head of a sister of α.[6] (Chomsky (1986: 15))

---

[6] The definition of θ-marking is as follows:
    α directly θ-marks β only if α and β are sisters.   (Chomsky (1986a: 14))

(11) Antecedent-government: X W-antecedent-governs Y (W={A, A', X^0}) iff
    (i) a. X is in a W-position
        b. X c-commands Y
    (ii) X and Y are coindexed
    (iii) a. no barrier intervenes
        b. Relativized Minimality is respected   (Rizzi (1990: 25))

(12) Relativized Minimality: X α-governs Y only if there is no Z such that
    (i) Z is a typical potential α-governor for Y
    (ii) Z c-commands Y and does not c-command X.   (Ibid.: 1990: 7)

Let us now examine how Rizzi's ECP predicts the ungrammaticality of the *that*-trace effect.

(13) a. *Who do you think that left   (Ibid.: 29)
    b. Who do you think left   (Ibid.: 51)

(13a) has the following representation at the level of S-Structure, where the *wh*-phrase *who* leaves its trace in Spec-C and Spec-I.

(14) Who do you think [$_{CP}$ t' [$_{C'}$ [$_C$ that] [$_{IP}$ t [$_{I'}$ I [$_{VP}$ left]]]]]

In (14), the intermediate trace in Spec-C antecedent-governs the original trace in Spec-I: no potential governors intervene between them. Thus, the second clause of the definition of the ECP in (8) is observed. However, the head-government requirement in the first clause of (8) is not observed: the original trace in Spec-I is not head-governed by C, which is not qualified as a head-governor by definition. Assuming that "proper head-government" is the requirement that an X^0 category govern a trace in its immediate projection, Rizzi (1990) then argues that I^0 does not properly head-govern the trace in Spec-I.

(15)

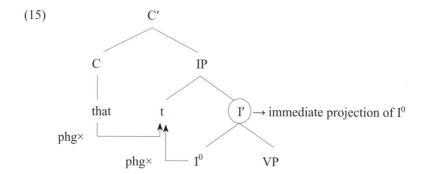

The immediate projection of I^0 in (15) is I', which makes it impossible for I^0 to properly head-govern the trace in Spec-I. Thus, (13a) violates both clauses of the ECP, and is ungrammatical.

Let us turn to (13b). The antecedent-government holds between the intermediate trace in Spec-C and the original trace in Spec-I, on a par with (13a)—no potential governors intervene between them. Thus, the second clause of the ECP in (8) is observed. Then, in order to rule in (13b), Rizzi (1990) argues that there are two types of tensed complementizer in English: one is an overt C, i.e., *that*, and the other a covert (or null) C, which consists of Agr.

(16) C → $\left\{ \begin{array}{l} that \\ Agr \end{array} \right\}$

Rizzi further argues that while overt C is inert for government, covert C becomes active and acquires governing capacity when a *wh*-operator lands in Spec-C. We then have the structures in (17a) and (17b) for (13a) and (13b), respectively.

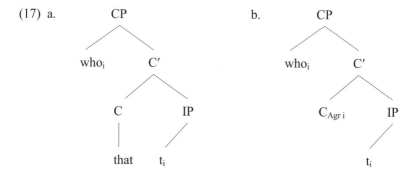

Chapter 3 Total Extraction 77

As discussed above, in (17a) the original trace in Spec-I is not properly head-governed. In contrast, in (17b), when the *wh*-operator *who* lands in Spec-C, it agrees with C_{Agr} in the configuration of the Spec-head relation, and as a result, C_{Agr} has the same index as the original trace in Spec-I, which makes it possible for C_{Agr} to head-govern the original trace. Thus, (16b) fulfills the first clause of the ECP in (8).

Let us next turn our attention to (7b) above, repeated below as (18).

(18) *Who do you prefer [$_{CP}$ t'$_{who}$ [$_{C'}$ for [t$_{who}$ to win]]]?

In order to exclude (18), the original trace in Spec-I needs to be an offending trace. As is usually assumed, the infinitival subject position, that is, Spec-I, is governed by the infinitival complementizer *for*, as seen in (19).

(19) John prefers [$_{CP}$ [$_{C'}$ [$_C$ for] [$_{IP}$ her to go]]].

In (19) the infinitival complementizer governs the infinitival subject and assigns oblique case to it. Given the structure of CP in (19), the infinitival complementizer is assumed to properly govern the trace in Spec-I, because the infinitival complementizer *for* is in the immediate projection of C^0, i.e., C′, as demonstrated in (20).

(20)

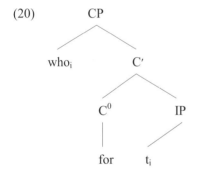

In (20), the trace in Spec-I is properly head-governed by C^0 and (18b) is predicted to be grammatical, which is not the case. Rizzi (1990), however, elaborates on the position of the infinitival complementizer *for*, claiming that it belongs to the P(reposition), which is dominated by C, as demonstrated in (21).

(21)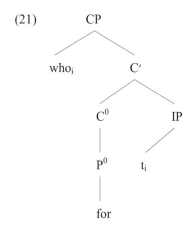

In (21), the immediate projection for the infinitival preposition is not C' but C^0. It then follows that the original trace in Spec-I cannot be properly head-governed, which makes the sentence ungrammatical. Notice here that *for* as P^0 can case-assign the subject in Spec-I, because contrary to government for the ECP, government for case-assignment does not need to occur under the immediate projection of a governor but can instead occur under m-command, as shown in (9).

3.1.3. Problems with Pre-Minimalist Analyses

In the previous two subsections, we have taken a brief overview of two analyses concerning overt complementizer effects, by Chomsky (1986) and Rizzi (1990) respectively. Although it seems easy to simply discard these two analyses because they depend on the notion of government, which should be dispensed with in the Minimalist Program, it is still worth considering some general problems in Chomsky's and Rizzi's analyses and their implications for the larger discussion.

One problem with Chomsky's analysis lies in the analysis of the null complementizer. Although he attributes the nonexistence of a C' projection to the assumption that a null head is featureless, this is not always so. For instance, the Infl (I) node in (22), which has no elements and is null, and featureless in the sense of Chomsky, but does have a feature that designates the subjunctive.

(22)   They demand [$_{CP}$ that [$_{IP}$ students [$_{I'}$ [$_{I}$] be punctual]]].

The analysis of featureless C brings out another problem. Chomsky claims that featureless null C does not give rise to a C' projection, which implies that featureless null C takes an IP as its complement to form a CP.

(23)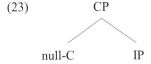

If this reasoning is correct, there are no intermediate landing sites for a *wh*-phrase because there is no room for Spec-C.

One may argue against our objection, claiming that the intermediate landing site of the *wh*-phrase is the adjunction site rather than Spec-C. However, this claim cannot be supported, because it does not obey the condition of Adjunction.

(24) Adjunction is possible only to a maximal projection (hence, X″) that is a nonargument. (Chomsky (1986a: 6))

The CP projection in (4a) and (7a), repeated below as (25), is an argument, since it is selected by the verb.

(25) a. Who would you believe [$_{CP}$ t′ [$_{C'}$ e [$_{IP}$ t would win]]]
 b. Who do you prefer [t$_{who}$ C [t$_{who}$ to win]]?

In order to retain Spec-C, C′ has to be projected even when the head C is empty.

Another problem concerns case-assignment of the subject DP in a complement clause. Observe the following sentences.

(26) a. John prefers [$_{CP}$ for her to go].
 b. John prefers [$_{CP}$ C^0 her to go].

In (26a), the infinitival subject is case-assigned by the infinitival complementizer *for*. In Chomsky's analysis, the featureless C^0 cannot qualify as a case-assigner, because it does not have any features. It would then follow that the matrix verb *prefer* case-assigns the infinitival subject. However, this reasoning cannot be maintained, because the CP precludes the V (*prefer*) from case-assigning the infinitival subject. Observe (27), where PRO occurs in the infinitival subject position.

(27) John prefers [$_{CP}$ C^0 PRO to go].

If the matrix V (*prefers*) case-assigns the infinitival subject, PRO will be impossible here. This problem seems to be rooted in the status of the null infinitival complementizer C^0.

Let us turn next to problems with Rizzi's (1990) analysis. One problem with Rizzi's ECP approach to overt complementizer effects is that it cannot explain the grammaticality of (7a) above, repeated here as (28).

(28) Who do you prefer to win?

Suppose that in (28) the infinitival clause consists of a projection of CP, whose specifier hosts the trace of a *wh*-phrase and whose head is empty infinitival C.

(29) a. Who do you prefer [$_{CP}$ t'[$_{C'}$ C [$_{TP}$ t to win]]]
     b.

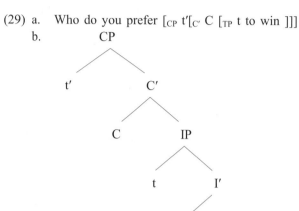

The original trace in Spec-I has to be subject to the head-government requirement. It cannot be head-governed by infinitival I, because it is not in the immediate projection of infinitival I. Similarly, the infinitival complementizer C does not qualify as a head-governor, because the complementizer in (29) is not tensed C. Rizzi (1990) claims that only a tensed null C has Agr features that can govern the subject trace in Spec-I. It can therefore be concluded that Rizzi's ECP approach cannot predict the grammaticality of (29).

Another problem with Rizzi's ECP approach can be found in its definition of "head-government requirement" in (9). As seen in (ib) under (9), the notion of "m-command" is required for Rizzi's analysis,[7] in order for the subject DP to be assigned nominative case by I(nfl). The requirement further makes the proper head-government requirement complicated: a trace be

---

[7] Besides the concern outlined in the text here, there is also the fact that there is no relation of "m-command" in the current Minimalist Program. See Chomsky (2004: 109) for further details.

governed within an immediate projection of a head-governor. This state of affairs leads to the complicated structure of the *for-to* infinitival-complement clause CP as seen in (30), where the head C^0 dominates P^0.

(30)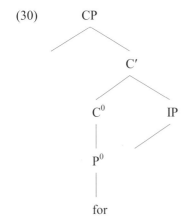

The proposed structure is in violation of X-bar theory, in that a head of a phrase has two heads.

In this subsection, we have discussed some problems with Chomsky's (1986) and Rizzi's (1990) ECP approaches to overt C-trace effects. The problem that these two analyses have in common is in their explanations of the structure of an infinitival clause with a lexical subject introduced with an infinitival complementizer *for*. This problem seems to make it difficult to account for overt C-trace effects.

In the next section, we will show how our Excorporation approach to subextraction of a *wh*-phrase from a subject accounts for the overt-complementizer effect, and further show that our analysis can explain the *that*- and *for*-trace effects in the same way without positing a special structure for the infinitival CP.

3.2. The Excorporation Analysis

This section will show how our Excorporation Analysis proposed in Chapter 2 analyzes overt/covert complementizer effects caused by total extraction of a *wh*-phrase. We will analyze *for*-and *that*-copy effects utilizing the Excorporation Analysis.[8]

3.2.1. *For*-Copy Effects

The phenomena to be analyzed in this subsection are given in (31). While in (31a) a *wh*-phrase *of which car* is subextracted from the infinitival subject, with its grammaticality unaffected, in (31b) a *wh*-phrase *who* undergoes total extraction from the infinitival subject, and its grammaticality is degraded.

(31) a. Of which major is it important [for the students of which major to take a course in physics]?
b. *Who is it important [for who to take a course in physics]?[9]

For the derivation of (31a), see 2.3.2. Here, we will begin with the embedded v*P phase in (31b). This phase has the following structure, where v*-V (*take*) is drawn from the lexicon as a lexical complex and merged with a complement DP, forming the VP.

(32)

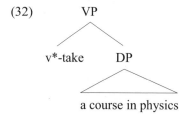

In the next stage of the derivation, v* excorporates and merges with the VP, forming the projection of v*, with an external argument *who* merged with this projection.

---

[8] We will use the terms "*for*-copy effect" and "*that*-copy effect" instead of "*for*-trace effect" and "*that*-trace effect" in this and following chapters.

[9] Material in outline font indicates that it is a copy.

Chapter 3 Total Extraction   83

(33)

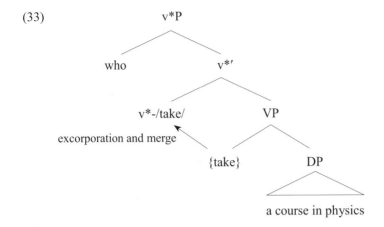

Remember that excorporation and merge of v* always accompanies the sound (phonetic form) of the main verb, represented as /take/ above, while a copy which consists of the meaning, represented as {...}, is left behind in the original position. Once all the expected operations are completed, the complement domain of the phase head (v*) undergoes the Transfer operation. In the next stage of the derivation, that is, the embedded CP phase, we have the following structures, where a lexical complex C-T (*for*)-M (*to*) is merged with v*P, to form the projection of M, i.e. the MP (Modal Phrase).

(34)

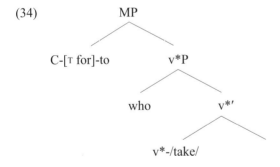

In the next stage of the derivation, C-[T *for*] excorporates and merges with the MP to form the projection of T.

(35)

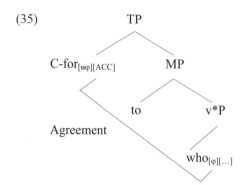

Recall here that the external argument *who* has valued φ-features and an unvalued case feature [...], while T (*for*) has unvalued φ-features and a case feature [ACC]. The agreement relation holds between T and the external argument *who* with respect to φ-features; as a result, the [uφ] of T are valued. The external argument *who*, which still has an unvalued case feature, undergoes Internal Merge (IM) to the projection of T, where the unvalued case feature [...] of the subject is valued as [ACC].[10]

(36)

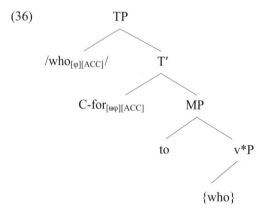

At the final stage of the derivation of the embedded CP phase, the null infinitival complementizer C excorporates and merges with TP, pied-piping *for* in accordance with the Overt Syntax Hypothesis.[11] Notice here that in this

---

[10] As proposed in 2.3.1, in English, case is assigned under Merge to the case-assigning category.

[11] The Overt Syntax Hypothesis is repeated here.
   Internal Merge must carry an element with a phonetic shape.

case, the null infinitival complementizer C has an uninterpretable focus feature [uF] that serves as a probe and locates a *wh*-phrase, which also has an interpretable counterpart.[12]

(37)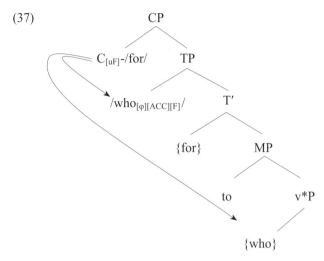

In (37), the infinitival complementizer C with [uF] locates two *wh*-phrases in its search space: one in Spec-T and the other in Spec-v*. However, attraction of the *wh*-phrase in Spec-v* is impossible, because as indicated by the curly brackets {...}, it consists of semantic features only, and not phonetic features. Attraction of elements with no phonetic features gives rise to violation of the Overt Syntax Hypothesis, as we saw in Chapter 2. The attraction of the other *wh*-phrase in Spec-T is also impossible, since the Revised Inactivity Condition (RIC) precludes it. (The RIC is repeated below.)

(38) Revised Inactivity Condition (RIC)
D and N that head the head of an A-chain become invisible to further computation when their uninterpretable features are valued.

Thus, the RIC states that D and N in a DP whose unvalued features are valued are invisible to further computation, but allows other elements than the D and N to remain intact.

(39) [$_{DP}$ D$_{[CASE]}$ [$_{NP}$ N$_{[CASE]}$ PP]]

---

[12] Regarding the focus feature that triggers Internal Merge of a *wh*-phrase, see the discussion in 2.3.3.

In (37), the interrogative *wh*-phrase *who* at the same time belongs to the D and constitutes a DP, and its unvalued case feature [...] is valued as [ACC]. Thus, it becomes invisible to further computation.

(40)   [$_{DP}$ who$_{[ACC]}$]

As seen above, this case valuation has already taken place before excorporation of C, which has [uF] that would attract a *wh*-phrase into its specifier position. We can therefore attribute the ungrammaticality of (31b) to the fact that the uninterpretable focus feature [uF] of C is not checked and deleted.

In this section, we have observed how our Excorporation Analysis, together with the Revised Inactivity Condition, can account for *for*-copy effects. Our analysis reduces *for*-copy effects to violations of the RIC. This explains these effects in a more natural way than Rizzi (1990), in that it does not posit a special structure of CP, in the head of which the prepositional complementizer is generated.

3.2.2. *That*-Copy Effects

We will now adapt our analysis of *for*-copy effects to *that*-copy effects, as exemplified in (41).

(41) a.   *Who do you think [$_{CP}$ that [$_{TP}$ who will see Mary]]
     b.   Who do you think [$_{CP}$ C [$_{TP}$ who will see Mary]]

We will analyze (41) one by one. Let us focus on the ungrammatical sentence in (41a) first. The simplest way to exclude (41a) is to analyze it in the same way as *for*-copy effect, that is, as discussed in the previous subsection, 3.2.1. In other words, the ungrammaticality of (41a) can be attributed to violation of the RIC. In order to implement such an analysis, we assume (42) in the CP phase of the finite CP introduced with an overt complementizer.

(42)   An overt complementizer *that* and T do not constitute a lexical complex.[13]

Let us now examine how the assumption (42) can account for the ungrammaticality of (41a). In the embedded v*P phase we have (43), where v*-V (*see*) is drawn from the lexicon as a lexical complex and merged with a

---

[13] We assume that the selectional relation between *that* and a finite T holds in the course of structure-building even if *that* and T do not constitute a lexical complex.

complement DP, forming a VP.

(43)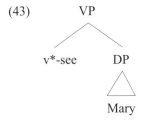

In the next stage of the derivation, v* excorporates and merges to VP, forming a projection of v*, with an external argument *who* merged with the projection. Notice that excorporation and merge of v* are executed carrying with them the phonetic shape of the main verb *see*, while the meaning of the main verb is left behind as a copy.

(44)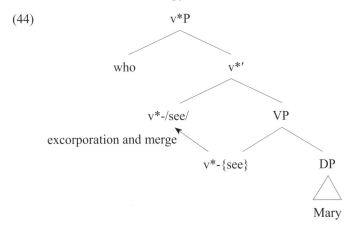

Needless to say, the complement domain VP is transferred when all the operations in this phase are completed.

Let us proceed to the embedded CP phase. We assume that the M(odal) here constitutes a lexical complex with T. Hence, In this case, the lexical complex T-*will* is drawn from the lexicon and merged with v*P, forming an MP.

(45)

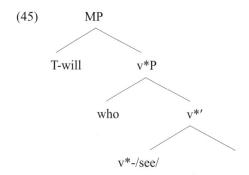

At the next stage of the derivation, T excorporates and merges with the MP to form a projection of T.

(46)

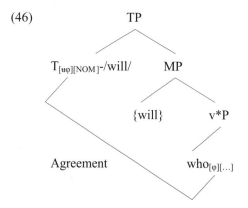

Recall here that the external argument *who* has valued φ-features and an unvalued case feature [...], while T has the corresponding unvalued φ-features and valued case feature [NOM]. The agreement relation thus holds between T and the external argument *who* with respect to φ-features. The external argument *who*, which still has the unvalued case feature, undergoes IM to the projection of T, where nominative case is assigned.

(47)

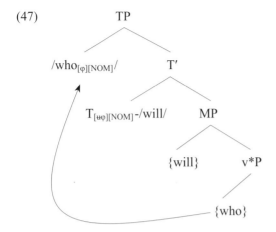

In (47), the interrogative subject *who* moves to Spec-T with its phonetic shape, represented as /who/, leaving its meaning, represented as {who}, behind in Spec-v*.

In the final stage of the derivation of the embedded CP phase, a complementizer *that* with an uninterpretable focus feature [uF] is merged to (47), in accordance with the assumption (42). Thus we have (48).

(48)

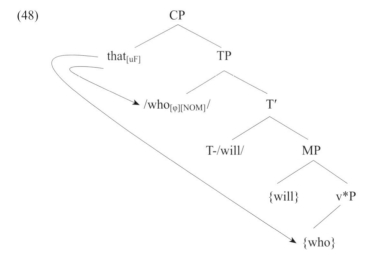

The complementizer *that* with [uF] in (48) serves as a probe and locates two *wh*-phrases in its search space: one in Spec-v* and the other in Spec-T. The attraction of the former is impossible for the same reason by now familiar: it does not have a phonetic shape. The IM of the latter to *that* with [uF]

90 On Extraction from Subjects

is also impossible, because the unvalued case feature [...] of the interrogative *wh*-phrase *who* is valued as [NOM] before merge of *that*. Now that the interrogative *wh*-phrase *who* is inactive, its IM violates the RIC. As a result, the uninterpretable focus feature [uF] of the overt C *that* is not checked and deleted, which makes (41a), repeated below as (49), ungrammatical.

(49) *Who do you think [$_{CP}$ that [$_{TP}$ who will see Mary]]

It can be concluded that our Excorporation Analysis, coupled with the assumption that an overt complementizer *that* does not constitute a lexical complex, successively reduces the ungrammaticality of *that*-copy effects (in traditional terms, *that*-trace effect) to a violation of the RIC.

Having seen how our analysis can account for *that*-copy effects, let us now turn our attention to their grammatical counterpart, that is, a sentence without *that*, as in (50).

(50) a. Who do you think will see Mary?
     b. Who do you think [$_{CP}$ C [$_{TP}$ who will see Mary]]?

If we make an attempt to derive (50) in the same way as we did above, (50) would be excluded for the reason that the movement of an interrogative *wh*-pronoun violates the RIC. To derive (50), we somehow have to move an inactive *wh*-phrase. Faced with this difficulty, we postulate a different derivation between embedded clauses with an overt complementizer *that* and those with a null complementizer C, and assume (51).

(51) An embedded null-C constitutes a lexical complex with T: C-T(-M).

With (51) in mind, let us turn back to the derivation of (50). Suppose that the derivation proceeds to the embedded CP phase, where the VP undergoes the Transfer operation and a lexical complex C-T-*will* is merged to v*P, forming the projection of M.

(52)

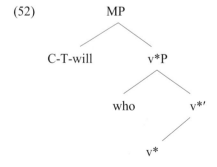

In the next stage of the derivation, the C-T complex excorporates and merges with MP, accompanying the phonetic form, /will/, and leaving the meaning, {will}.

(53)

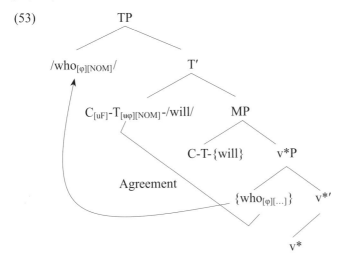

Recall that T and the subject *who* have [uφ][NOM] and [φ][...], respectively, and that the agreement relation holds between T and the subject with respect to φ-features. Furthermore, T with [NOM] attracts the subject from Spec-v* to Spec-T, and as a result the subject is assigned a [NOM] case. Before proceeding to the next stage of the derivation, it is worth pointing out that the null complementizer C has [uF]. A goal of the next stage of the derivation will be to build a CP structure that will be selected by the main verb *think*. There seem to be several possible derivations that achieve this goal: (i) excorporation of C alone and merge to TP; (ii) excorporation of a C-T complex and merge to TP; (iii) excorporation of a C-T-/will/; (iv) doing nothing. The first two options are excluded by the Overt Syntax Hypothesis, because excorporation and subsequent merge of C or a lexical complex C-T do not accompany a phonetic shape. Although the third option, excorporation and subsequent merge of a lexical complex C-T-/will/, obeys the Overt Syntax Hypothesis, the resulting derivation and structures makes it impossible for the *wh*-phrase *who* to be attracted further.

(54)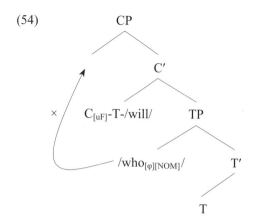

Although in (54), C has [uF] and serves as a probe and locates a *wh*-phrase in Spec-T, it cannot attract the *wh*-phrase, which is inactive; and attraction of an inactive element is in violation of the RIC. Then, the final option is (iv), doing nothing. Recall the discussion of the dual categorial status of a sentence in 2.3.1. Tonoike (2008a) argues that if C does not have unvalued features to be checked in TP, it does not undergo excorporation and subsequent merge to TP to form the projection of C. Thus, at this point for (54), it is worth examining the properties of C and the *wh*-phrase. Recall that in Chapter 2 we assumed along with Tonoike (2000) that *wh*-movement is driven by a focus feature [F] rather than a *wh*-feature, and that a focus feature [F] is involved in this movement. For instance, the DP in (55), which contains a *wh*-phrase, has the following structure.

(55) a. [$_{DP}$ [F] the driver [$_{PP}$ [F]of [$_{DP}$ [F] which$_{[Wh]}$ car]]]
    b. [$_{DP}$ [F] who$_{[Wh]}$]]

As argued by Tonoike (2008a), the focus feature [F] is optionally assigned to Spec-D and Spec-P in (55), and the function of [wh] feature is to identify a *wh*-word. Depending on which specifier position a [wh] feature is assigned to, the Focus-moved phrase is determined accordingly. In our case, a simple *wh*-word has the structure of (55b), in which [F] is assigned to Spec-D and a *wh*-word intrinsically has a [wh] feature. Phase heads, namely C and v*, also have a focus feature [F] but in this case it is an uninterpretable [uF]. In Chapter 2, we implicitly assume that this uninterpretable feature is checked and deleted by a *wh*-phrase that is moved into the specifier position of the phase head; that is, we assume that uninterpretable focus feature [uF] is similar to the case feature [NOM] of T, in that it triggers movement into its specifier position; in other words, it brings out the EPP effect.

Adopting this assumption concerning the focus feature, let us now turn to the embedded CP phase in (53), where the interrogative *wh*-subject is attracted to Spec-T from Spec-v* for case-theoretic reasons, as shown below.

(56)

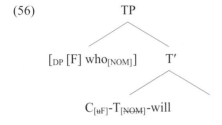

In (56), the *wh*-phrase *who* is case-assigned, and the [NOM] of T is checked and deleted. It is also possible for [F] of the *wh*-phrase to check and delete the [uF] of C because these two elements are in a Spec-head configuration. The uninterpretable features of C and T are checked and deleted, which means that the lexical complex C-T-/*will*/ does not undergo excorporation and subsequent merge. This analysis further implies that the categorial status of the topmost projection of the embedded clause is not only CP but also TP.

(57)

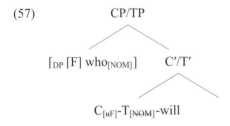

In (57), then, the embedded clause introduced with a null complementizer C has a dual syntactic category: CP and IP.

Armed with this established dual categorial status of the embedded clause, let us go on to analyze a sentence that obviates *that*-copy effects. In the matrix v*P phase, a lexical complex v*-V (*think*) is merged to (57). The categorial status of the embedded clause at this time is CP; otherwise, the selectional property of the matrix verb would not be satisfied. The lexical complex v*-*think* excorporates and merges with the VP, with a subject of the matrix clause *you* merged to the projection of v*.

On Extraction from Subjects

(58)

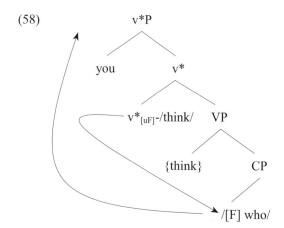

In (58), v* has an uninterpretable focus feature [uF], and serves as a probe, locating a *wh*-phrase in Spec-C and attracting it to Spec-v*. Worthy of noticing here is that the *wh*-phrase is in Spec-C rather than Spec-T; or more precisely, seen from the inside of the embedded clause the *wh*-phrase is in Spec-T, but seen from the matrix v*P phase it is in Spec-C. This implies that seen from v*, the *wh*-phrase heads the A-bar-chain rather than the A-chain, which in turn means that the attraction of the *wh*-phrase in Spec-C to Spec-v* does not violate the RIC (repeated here as (59)).

(59) Revised Inactivity Condition (RIC)
D and N that head the head of an A-chain become invisible to further computation when their uninterpretable features are valued.

The RIC is thus sensitive to A-chain rather than the A-bar-chain; and as the derivation proceeds to the matrix CP, the interrogative *wh*-phrase is attracted to the matrix Spec-C by the uninterpretable [uF] of the matrix C.

(60) [$_{CP}$ /$_{DP}$ [F] Who/ [$_{C'}$ C$_{[uF]}$-T-do [$_{TP}$ you [$_{MP}$ [$_{v*P}$ {who} ...

The assumption that the null C constitutes a lexical complex with T and that a null C and T that have no uninterpretable features to be checked project both a CP and a TP at the same time, makes it possible to move an interrogative *wh*-phrase without incurring violation of the RIC.

Before summarizing this section, let us reexamine the derivation of (57). One may argue against our analysis of dual categorial status that the same effect can be obtained by excorporation and subsequent merge of C with TP followed by IM of a *wh*-phrase to Spec-C, where the uninterpretable focus feature [uF] is checked and deleted.

(61)

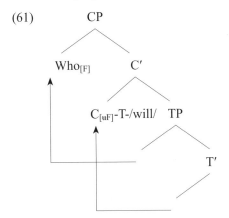

However, this derivation is excluded by the Principle of Economy and the RIC. First, (57) is more economical than (61) in that (57) is derived by fewer operations than (61). Second, the attraction of *who* to Spec-C from Spec-T is prohibited by the RIC, because the *wh*-phrase in Spec-T heads an A-chain with [NOM] assigned in Spec-T.

To sum up this section, we posit different derivations for (41), which is repeated below as (62).

(62) a. *Who do you think [$_{CP}$ that [$_{TP}$ who will see Mary]]
b. Who do you think [$_{CP/TP}$ who C-will see Mary]

While the overt complementizer *that* does not constitute a lexical complex with the lexical complex T-M (*will*) in the embedded CP phase of (62a), the covert complementizer C does constitute a lexical complex with T-M (*will*), namely C-T-M, in the embedded CP phase of (62b). This analysis makes it possible for (62a) to be excluded by the RIC while enabling us to posit dual categorial status of the embedded clause in (62b), by which the *wh*-phrase is successively raised.

3.2.3. Extraction from an Infinitival Subject of the Complement Clause of *want*

In this subsection, we will analyze the total extraction and subextraction of a *wh*-phrase from a subject of the infinitival complement clause of the verb *want*. The data to be analyzed are as follows.

(63) a. Of which car do you want the driver to avoid an accident?
b. Of which car do you want very much for a driver to avoid an accident?

(64) a. Who do you want to avoid an accident?
b. *Who do you want very much for to avoid an accident?

Before analyzing (63) and (64), we must examine the structure of the infinitival complement of *want*-class verbs with a lexical subject. Bach (1977), Lasnik and Saito (1991), and Bošković (1995) persuasively show that the infinitival complement of *want* is a CP rather than a TP. Consider (65), which involves anaphor-binding.

(65) a. ?I believed those men to be unreliable because of each other's statement.
b.??*I wanted those men to be fired because of each other's statements.

The grammaticality difference found between the two sentences in (65) leads us to conclude that whereas the ECM complement is TP, the infinitival complement of *want* is CP. Assuming that the adverbial phrase in (65) is adjoined to the intermediate projection of the main verb, it can be concluded that while *those men* in (65a) is raised higher than the adverbial phrase and binds the reciprocal pronoun, in (65b) it stays in situ, as result of which the reciprocal pronoun is not bound. (As argued in Chapter 1, an ECM subject is raised to Spec-V for case-theoretic reasons.)[14]

---

[14] We will analyze the derivation and structure of ECM in terms of the Excorporation Aanalysis in more detail in Chapter 4.

Chapter 3   Total Extraction   97

(66) a.

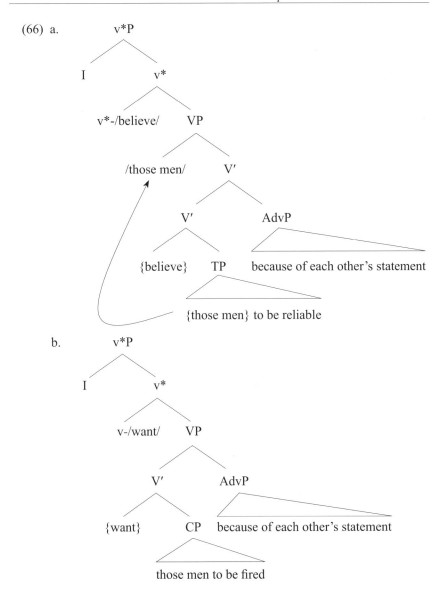

Those men in (66a) c-commands the reciprocal pronoun *each other*, but that in (66b) does not.

A question now arises concerning the detailed structure and derivation of an infinitival-complement CP of *want*-class verbs. As is well known, an infinitival-complement CP of *want* is introduced with the overt complementizer *for* when an adverbial element intervenes between the verb and the lexical subject of the complement clause.

(67) a. I want very much for him to win the race.
  b. I want him to win the race.

We will first analyze (67a) in terms of excorporation. Recall that in Chapter 2 we proposed that the so-called infinitival *for* belongs to T and constitutes a lexical complex with C and M (*to*). Thus, at an early stage of derivation of the embedded CP phase of (67a), we have the following configuration, where the lexical complex C-*for-to* is merged with v*P, forming an MP.

(68) [$_{MP}$ C-for$_{[ACC]}$-to [$_{v*P}$ him$_{[...]}$ v*-/win/ [$_{VP}$ {win} the race]]]

In the next stage of the derivation, the lexical complex C-*for* excorporates and merges with MP to form a TP, and the infinitival lexical subject is raised to Spec-T for case-theoretic reasons.

(69) [$_{TP}$ /him$_{[ACC]}$/ [$_{T'}$ C-for$_{[ACC]}$ [$_{MP}$ to [$_{v*P}$ {him} v*-/win/]]]]

In the final stage of the derivation of the embedded CP phase, the lexical complex excorporates and merges with the TP, to form a projection of C.[15]

(70) [$_{CP}$ C-/for/[$_{TP}$ /him$_{[ACC]}$/ [$_{T'}$ {for} [$_{MP}$ to [$_{v*P}$ {him} v*-/win/]]]]]

Let us now turn to the derivation and structure of (67b). Here, as shown in (71), the lexical complex C-T$_{[ACC]}$-*to* is merged with the projection of v*, to form MP. We assume here that the null T has an accusative case feature [ACC].

(71) [$_{MP}$ C-T$_{[ACC]}$-to [$_{v*P}$ him$_{[...]}$ v*-/win/ [$_{VP}$ {win} the race]]]

The lexical complex C-T$_{[ACC]}$ must excorporate and merge to MP, forming TP; otherwise, the lexical infinitival subject cannot be assigned an accusative case, because we assume that case is assigned under Merge to the case-assigning category: M(odal) is not a case-assigning category. Excorporation is implemented, pied-piping *to* (M) because IM always includes sound (phonetic form) in our framework, in accordance with the Overt Syntax Hypothesis.[16]

---

[15] As to the reason for excorporation of the lexical complex C-*for*, see footnote 25 in Chapter 2.

[16] The Overt Syntax Hypothesis is as follows.
  Internal Merge must carry an element with a phonetic shape.

(72) [TP /him_{[ACC]}/ [T' C-T_{[ACC]}-/to/ [MP {to} [v*P {him} v*-/win/]]]]

Worth noticing here is that, in contrast with the derivation observed in (69) and (70), in (72) the lexical complex C-T does not undergo further excorporation or subsequent merge because C and T contain no uninterpretable features and no phonetic shapes; this means that the topmost projection of (72) is not only TP but also CP.[17]

(73) [CP/TP /him_{[ACC]}/ [C'/T' C-T_{[ACC]}-/to/ [MP {to} [v*P {him} v*-/win/]]]]

Having observed the structure and derivation of the infinitival-complement CP of *want*, let us turn to (63) and (64), repeated below as (74) and (75).

(74) a. Of which car do you want the driver to avoid an accident?
b. Of which car do you want very much for a driver to avoid an accident?

(75) a. Who do you want to avoid an accident?
b. *Who do you want very much for to avoid an accident?

We will first analyze (74a) and (75a). Let us begin with the embedded v*P phase, where the lexical subject is merged with the projection v*' and the complement domain VP is transferred.

(76) a. [v*P the driver of which car [v*' v*-/avoid/ [VP {avoid} an accident]]]
b. [v*P who [v*' v*-/avoid/ [VP {avoid} an accident]]]

In the embedded CP phase, C-T_{[ACC]}-M (*to*) is merged with (76), forming an MP.

(77) a. [MP C-T_{[ACC]}-to [v*P the_{[...]} driver of which car [v*' v*-/avoid/]]]
b. [MP C-T_{[ACC]}-to [v*P who_{[...]} [v*' v*-/avoid/]]]

In the next stage of the derivation, C-T_{[ACC]} excorporates and merges with MP, with a phonetic shape of /to/ pied-piped, to project TP, and the lexical subject raised to Spec-T for case-theoretic reasons.

---

[17] The selectional property of the matrix verb *want* is satisfied because seen from the position of the matrix predicate, the categorial status of the embedded clause is that of CP. As to its dual categorial status, see 3.2.2 for details.

(78) a. [TP /the[ACC] driver of which car/ [T' C-T_for [ACC]-/to/ [MP {to} [v*P {the driver of which car} [v*' v*-/avoid/]]]]]
b. [TP /who[ACC]/ [T' C-T_for [ACC]-/to/ [MP {to} [v*P {who} [v*' v*-/avoid/]]]]]

Remember the discussion on the categorial status of the topmost projection in (78). Here there are no uninterpretable features to drive excorporation of C-T[ACC], which in turn means that the categorial status of the projection is, again, not only TP but also CP.[18]

(79) a. [CP/TP /the[ACC] driver of which car/ [C'/T' C-T[ACC]-/to/ [MP {to} [v*P {the driver of which car} [v*' v*-/avoid/]]]]]
b. [CP/TP /who[ACC]/ [C'/T' C-T[ACC]-/to/ [MP {to} [v*P {who} [v*' v*-/avoid/]]]]]

From this point, (79a) and (79b) will have slightly different derivations. We will look at (79a) first. Recall the discussion concerning *wh*-movement in 2.3.3 as well as in previous sections of this chapter, where we assume that a phrase which undergoes *wh*-movement must be assigned an interpretable focus feature [F]. In (81a), [F] is assigned to Spec-P in the subject DP.

(80) [DP the[ACC] driver [PP [F] of [which car]]]

Suppose that the derivation proceeds to the matrix v*P phase, where a lexical complex v*-*want* is merged with (79a), followed by excorporation and merge of v*-/want/ to form a projection of v*, with which the subject is merged. The v* part of the lexical complex is assigned an uninterpretable [uF] to be checked and deleted.

(81) [v*P you [v*' v*[uF]-/want/ [VP very much {want} [CP/TP /the[ACC] driver [PP [F]of which car]/ [C'/T' C-T_for[ACC]-/to/ [MP {to} [v*P {the driver of which car} [v*' v*-/avoid/]]]]]]]][19, 20]

In (81) v*[uF] serves as a probe and locates a PP in the DP, as a result of which the PP is attracted to outer Spec-v*.

---

[18] Even if C has an uninterpretable feature to be checked by the subject *wh*-phrase, it is possible to check it in the configuration of (78).

[19] We tentatively assume that *very much* is adjoined to the embedded VP.

[20] We assume that MP, which is a complement domain of C-T, undergoes the transfer operation.

(82) [$_{v*P}$ [$_{PP}$ [F] /of which car/] [$_{v*'}$ you [$_{v*'}$ v*$_{[uF]}$-/want/ [$_{VP}$ very much {want} [$_{CP/TP}$ /the$_{[ACC]}$ driver {$_{PP}$ of which car}/ [$_{C'/T'}$ C-T$_{for\ [ACC]}$ /to/]]]]]]]

Attracting the PP *of which car* does not violate the RIC, since it states that what is frozen in place is a D or N, not a PP. As a result of the movement of the PP, the uninterpretable [uF] of v* is checked and deleted. Then, the final stage of the derivation, the PP *of which car* is attracted to the matrix Spec-C.

(83) [$_{CP}$ [$_{PP}$ F] /of which car/] [$_{C'/T'}$ C$_{[uF]}$-T-/do/ [$_{TP}$ /you/ [$_{MP}$ [$_{v*P}$ {of which car} [$_{v*'}$ {you} [$_{v*'}$ v*$_{[uF]}$-/want/ [$_{VP}$ very much {want} [$_{CP/TP}$ /the$_{[ACC]}$ driver {$_{PP}$ of which car}/ [$_{T'}$ C-T$_{for\ [ACC]}$ /to/]]]]]]]]]

Having examined the derivation of (74a), let us return to (79b(=75a)), repeated below as (84).

(84) [$_{CP/TP}$ /who$_{[ACC]}$/ [$_{T'}$ C-T $_{[ACC]}$-/to/ [$_{MP}$ {to} [$_{v*P}$ {who} [$_{v*'}$ v*-/avoid/]]]]]

In the case of (84), an interpretable [F] is assigned to Spec-D of the subject DP.

(85) [$_{DP}$ [F] [$_D$ who$_{[ACC]}$]]

Suppose that the derivation proceeds to the matrix v*P phase, where v*-*want* is merged with (84) to form a projection of the V, followed by excorporation and merge of v*-*want* with VP.

(86) [$_{v*P}$ you [$_{v*'}$ v*$_{[uF]}$-/want/ [$_{VP}$ {want} [$_{CP/TP}$ /who$_{[ACC]}$/ [$_{C'/T''}$ C-T$_{[ACC]}$-/to/ [$_{MP}$ {to} [$_{v*P}$ {who} [$_{v*'}$ v*-/avoid/]]]]]]]]

In (86) the subject is generated in Spec-v*, and v* is assigned an uninterpretable focus feature [uF], which serves as a probe and locates an interrogative *wh*-phrase *who*. It then follows that *who* is attracted to Spec-v*. The movement of *who* from the infinitival clause into Spec-v* would appear to violate the RIC, which bans a case-assigned element from being moved. However, this does not prove to be the case with (86). As discussed in 3.2.2, seen from the matrix v*, the *wh*-interrogative phrase here is in Spec-C, not Spec-T, which in turn means that it is the head of an A-bar chain, not an A-chain. Thus, the interrogative *wh*-phrase *who* in (86) is immune to the RIC and as a result can move into Spec-v*.

(87) [$_{v*P}$ /[F] who$_{[ACC]}$/ [$_{v*'}$ you [$_{v*'}$ v*$_{[uF]}$-/want/ [$_{VP}$ {want} [$_{CP/TP}$ {who} [$_{C'/T''}$ C-T$_{for\ [ACC]}$-/to/ [$_{MP}$ {to} [$_{v*P}$ {who} [$_{v*'}$ v*-/avoid/]]]]]]]]]

It can be concluded that our Excorporation Analysis can deal with the extraction of a *wh*-phrase from an infinitival complement of *want* introduced without an overt complementizer *for*.

Now let us turn to (74b) and (75b), which are repeated below as (88).

(88) a. Of which car do you want very much for the driver to avoid an accident?
b. *Who do you want very much for to avoid an accident?

The entire embedded clauses in (88) have the same structure and derivation, so we will analyze them at the same time. In the embedded v*P phase, a lexical complex v*-*avoid* merges with the complement DP, followed by excorporation and subsequent merge of the lexical complex to form a projection of v*, with which the external argument is merged.

(89) a. [$_{v*P}$ the driver of which car [$_{v*'}$ v*-/avoid/ [$_{VP}$ {avoid} an accident]]]
b. [$_{v*P}$ who [$_{v*'}$ v*-/avoid/ [$_{VP}$ {avoid} an accident]]]

In (89), the VP undergoes the Transfer operation. In the embedded CP phase, the lexical complex C-*for-to* is merged with (89), to form an MP. In this case, *for* has the uninterpretable case feature [ACC].

(90) a. [$_{MP}$ C-for$_{[ACC]}$-to [$_{v*P}$ the$_{[...]}$ driver of which car [$_{v*'}$ v*-/avoid/]]]
b. [$_{MP}$ C-for$_{[ACC]}$-to [$_{v*P}$ who$_{[...]}$ [$_{v*'}$ v*-/avoid/]]]

In the next stage of the derivation, C-*for* excorporates and merges with the MP, to form a projection of T, to whose specifier the lexical subject is attracted; as a result, the unvalued case feature of the lexical subject [...] is valued as [ACC].

(91) a. [$_{TP}$ /the$_{[ACC]}$ driver of which car/ [$_{T'}$ C-for$_{[ACC]}$ [$_{MP}$ to [$_{v*P}$ {the driver of which car} [$_{v*'}$ v*-/avoid/]]]]]
b. [$_{TP}$ /who$_{[ACC]}$/ [$_{T'}$ C-for$_{[ACC]}$ [$_{MP}$ to [$_{v*P}$ {who}[$_{v*'}$ v*-/avoid/]]]]]

In the next stage of the derivation, the lexical complex C-*for* excorporates and merges with the TP, to form a projection of C. Recall that the subject phrases in (91) are assigned [F]: Spec-P in (91a) and Spec-D in (91b). Let us assume also that in (91) C is assigned [uF].

(92) a. [CP C[uF]-for [TP /the[ACC] driver [PP [F]of which car]/ [T' {for} [MP to [v*P {the driver of which car} [v*' v*-/avoid/]]]]]
b. [CP C[uF]-for [TP /[F] who[ACC]/ [T' {for} [MP to [v*P {who}[v*' v*-/avoid/]]]]]

In (92), C with [uF] serves as a probe and locates *of which car* in (92a) and *who* in (92b). In order for the uninterpretable focus feature [uF] to be checked and deleted, *of which car* and *who* must be moved to Spec-C. The RIC prohibits *who*, which is case-assigned, from being moved, but permits *of which car* to be moved, since the RIC is sensitive to the D and N, which are case-assigned. Thus, our Excorporation Analysis can successfully derive (88a) and exclude (88b).

3.3. Rizzi and Shlonsky (2007)

In this section, our analysis will be examined in comparison with that of Rizzi and Shlonsky (2007). In 3.3.1 we will introduce their analysis of subject extraction, based on their Subject Criterion. In 3.2.2, it will be demonstrated how they analyze the overt complementizer copy (trace) effect.

3.3.1. The Subject Criterion

Working with data from French and Italian as well as English, Rizzi and Shlonsky (2007) elaborate an account of subject-object asymmetries such as that in (93) within the framework of the Minimalist Program, which they argue is free from the pitfalls of the ECP approach.

(93) a. *Qui crois-tu que t_{qui} va gagner?
'Who do you believe that will win?'
(Rizzi and Shlonsky (2007: 115))
b. Qui crois-tu que Paul va aider t_{qui}?
'Who do you believe that Paul will help?' (Ibid.)

The French complementizer *que* is impossible when a subject is extracted but possible when an object is extracted. The ECP approach excludes (93a) because the trace left behind by subject extraction cannot be properly governed: *que* does not function as a proper governor, and the trace is not in the immediate projection of I (T). (For basic discussion of the ECP in this context, see 3.1.) In contrast, object traces always undergo proper government by their verbs. Claiming that it is difficult to reanalyze ECP in terms of Minimalism, Rizzi and Shlonsky (2007) make an attempt to account for the subject-object asymmetry in (93) in terms of Criterial Freezing. We are now in a position to review their Criterial Freezing.[21] Observe (94) below.

(94) a. Pensavo che avessero scelto la RAGAZZA, non il ragazzo
'I thought they had chosen the GIRL, not the boy'
b. La RAGAZZA pensavo che avessero scelto ___ , non il ragazzo.
'The GIRL I thought they had chosen ___ , not the boy'
(Rizzi and Shlonsky (2007: 117))

Above, (94) shows that in Italian a focal element can optionally undergo focus movement. However, such an element cannot undergo focus movement if it is contained within a larger *wh*-phrase in Spec-C.

(95) a. Mi domandava quale RAGAZZA avessero, non quale ragazzo.
'I wondered which GIRL they had chosen, not which boy'
b. *Quale RAGAZZA mi domandavo avessero scelto, non qale ragazzo
'Which GIRL I wondered they had chosen, not which boy.'
(Ibid.: 117)

Whereas in (95a), a focused element *RAGAZZA* is contained in the *wh*-phrase *quale RAGAZZA*, which undergoes *wh*-movement to Spec-C, in (95b) it undergoes further focus movement, and the grammaticality is degraded. In order to account for this fact, Rizzi (2004) proposes Criterial Freezing, represented in (96) below.

(96) Criterial Freezing
An element moved to a position dedicated to some scope-discourse interpretive property, a criterial position, is frozen in place.
(Ibid.: 116)

In (95a), the phrase *quale RAGAZZA* becomes frozen when it moves to the embedded Spec-C, which is a criterial position dedicated to the scope-interpretive property. Thus, after this, further focus movement gives rise to ungrammaticality, as shown in (95b).

Rizzi (2004) argues that Criterial Freezing in (96) cannot be satisfied "in passing." Suppose that we have an intermediate sentence structure where a complex *wh*-phrase *quanti librir del quale* ('how many books by whom'), is situated in Spec-C.

---

[21] On Criterial Freezing, see also Rizzi (2007).

(97)   Gianni, [___ C$_{REL}$ [non è ancora stato chiarito [[quanti librir del quale] C$_Q$ [siano stati censurati t$_{DP}$]]]]
'Gianni, it has not been clarified yet how many books by whom have been censored.'

As predicted by Criterial Freezing (96), it is impossible for a complex *wh*-phrase that contains a relative pronoun to undergo relativization, as illustrated in (98).

(98)   *Gianni, [[quanti librir del quale] C$_{REL}$ [non è ancora stato chiarito [t$_{DP}$ C$_Q$ [siano stati censurati t$_{DP}$]]]]
'Gianni, how many books by whom it has not been clarified yet have been censored'

However, both subextraction of a *wh*-relative pronoun out of the complex *wh*-interrogative phrase, yielding (99a), and pied-piping of a whole interrogative clause into Spec-C$_{REL}$, as represented in (99b), are possible.

(99) a.   Gianni, [del quale C$_{REL}$ [non è ancora stato chiarito [[quanti libri t$_{PP}$] C$_Q$ [siano stati censurati t$_{DP}$]]]]
'Gianni, by whom it has not been clarified yet how many books have been censored'
   b.   Gianni, [[[quanti libri del quale] C$_Q$ [siano stati censurati t$_{DP}$]] C$_{REL}$ [non è ancora stanto chiaritio t$_{CP}$]]
'Gianni, how many books by whom have been censored, it has not been clarified yet'

In (99a), it is *quanti libri* that satisfies the criterion, and so it is possible to subextract the relative pronoun *del quale*. The derivation of (99b) is complex: first, the embedded CP undergoes clausal pied-piping into Spec-C$_{REL}$, satisfying the requirement of Criterial Freezing imposed by C$_{REL}$; and second, the Q criterion is satisfied by the movement of the complex *wh*-phrase *quanti libri del quale* inside the fronted clause. In order to rule in (99), Rizzi and Shlonsky (2007) revised the Freezing Criterion as in (100), below.

(100)   Criterial Freezing
A phrase meeting a criterion is frozen in place.

They make an attempt to extend the analysis demonstrated above to the subject-object asymmetries found in (93) above. In the analysis they try to apply, the ungrammaticality of (93a) is triggered by violation of a criterion that holds between a subject and a head hosting the subject to its Spec. As a first attempt, they adopt the criterion for a subject, based on the criterion proposed in (Rizzi (1996, 1997)).

(101) Classical EPP, the requirement that clauses have subjects, can be restated as a criterial requirement, the Subject Criterion, formally akin to the Topic Criterion, the Focus Criterion, the Q or Wh Criterion, etc. (Rizzi (2006: 116))

In order to implement the Subject Criterion (101), Rizzi and Shlonsky (2007) modifies the sentence structure, proposing that there is a head that attracts a subject generated predicate-internally, which they term "Subj," and that this head is generated above T. Although he does not explicitly make this point, the head Subj consists of Agreement features, or φ-features.[22]

(102)

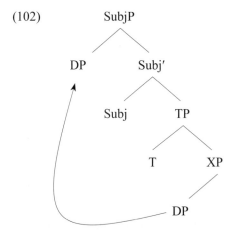

Assuming the Subject Criterion in (101) and Rizzi and Shlonsky's modified sentence structure in (102), let us see how the analysis by Rizzi and Shlonsky predicts the (un)grammaticality of (93), which is repeated, as (103), below.

(103) a. *Qui crois-tu que t_{qui} va gagner?
       'Who do you believe that will win?'
   b. Qui crois-tu que Paul va aider t_{qui}?
       'Who do you believe that Paul will help?'

---

[22] Rizzi (2012), following Chomsky (2013), argues that the projection that hosts the subject from the VP internal position is φP, and that its head consists of agreement features.

Above, (103a) is excluded because that the Subject Criterion is violated: when the interrogative subject *qui* is attracted to Spec-Subj, it is frozen in place. In contrast, the Subject Criterion is not in effect in (103b), due to the fact that an object *wh*-phrase does not move to Spec-Subj.

(104) a. Qui$_i$ crois-tu [$_{CP}$ que [$_{SubjP}$ t_{qui}* [$_{Subj'}$ Subj [t_{qui} va gagner]]]]?
     b. Qui crois-tu [$_{CP}$ que [$_{SubjP}$ Paul [$_{Subj'}$ Subj [va aider t_{qui}]]]]?

It is true that the Subject Criterion, together with the novel sentence structure, can account for the paradigm observed in (103) above, but there are constructions that allow *wh*-subjects to be extracted.

(105) a. *Quelle étudiante crois-tu [*t* que [*t* va partir]]?
        'Which student do you believe that is going to leave?
     b. Quelle étudiante crois-tu [*t* qui [*t* va partir]]?
        'Which student do you believe QUI is going to leave?
                                        (Ibid.: 131)

Above, (105a) is excluded in the same way as (104a): when *quelle étudiante* moves to Spec-Subj, it becomes frozen in place. However, the situation is complicated in (105b). As is well known, a *wh*-subject can be extracted if *que* turns into *qui*. Thus, (105b) is grammatical in spite of the fact that the subject is extracted from the criterial position Spec-Subj. In order to overcome this difficulty, Rizzi and Shlonsky (2007) propose "skipping strategies" as in (106) below.

(106)   Skipping Strategies
       The subject moves, but it is allowed to skip the freezing position and is extracted directly from its thematic position or from some other predicate-internal position.   (Ibid.: 119)

To implement (106), Rizzi and Shlonsky (2007) first reanalyze the *que-qui* alternation. According to the traditional analyses by Taraldsen (1978), Pesetsky (1982), and Rizzi (1990), among others, *qui* is derived from *que* when it agrees with a *wh*-subject.[23] However, Rizzi and Shlonsky, based on the "expletive analysis" by Taraldsen (2001),[24] propose instead that *qui* consists of *que* and -*i*, the former belonging to a complementizer and the latter, another type of complementizer, Fin, and that Fin -*i* has an unvalued number

---

[23] Rizzi (1990) analyzes *qui* as *que*+Agr.
[24] Taraldsen (2001) argues that *qui* is *que*+Expletive.

feature [αpl].[25]

Taking (107) as an example, let us observe how such an analysis explains *que-qui* alternation.

(107) l'homme qui va partir
'the man qui is going to leave'

In the early stage of this derivation, (107) has the following structure, where a relative operator is generated predicate-internally.

(108) [$_{FinP}$ [$_{Fin}$ -i][$_{SubjP}$ Subj [$_{AgrP}$ Agr [va [Rel-OP partir]]]]]

Here, the relative operator moves to Spec-FinP via Spec-Agr from the base-generated position, valuing the unvalued number feature α of Fin -*i* as "-" (minus).

(109)

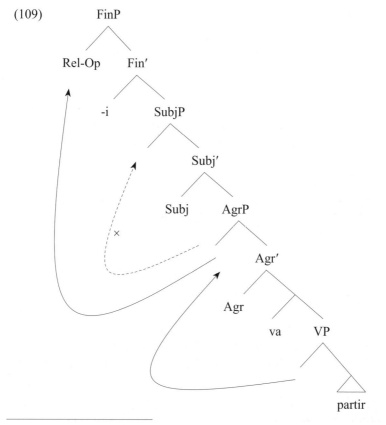

---

[25] "α" and "pl" in [αpl] represent "unspecified value" and "plural," respectively.

Notice here that the movement of Rel-Op skips Spec-Subj, which is a potential landing site and a criterial position for a subject; otherwise, Rel-Op could not move to Spec-C$_{Rel}$.

In the next stage of the derivation, *que*, which belongs to C$_{Rel}$, is merged with FinP, forming a projection of C to whose specifier the Rel-Op moves.

(110)   l'homme [$_{CP}$ Rel-Op$_i$ que [t_i $_{FinP}$ -*i* [$_{Subj}$ Subj [$_{AgrP}$ t_i Agr [va [t_i partir
(Ibid.: 136)

A problem emerges here as to how the Subject Criterion is satisfied in (107). As mentioned above, the Rel-Op cannot be situated in Spec-Subj, and so there are no elements to satisfy the Subject Criterion in the Spec-head configuration. Given this state of affairs, adopting the proposal by Rizzi (2004), Rizzi and Shlonsky claims that Subject Criterion is satisfied via a head-head relation as well as the Spec-head relation.

(111)   For [+F] a criterial feature, X_{+F} is locally c-commanded by A_{+F}.
(Ibid.: 139)

In this case, the licensing head is Fin, whose unvalued feature is valued by the subject Rel-Op, whereas in (107), the Subject Criterion is satisfied in terms of the c-command relation holding between Fin, which carries the relevant feature of subject, and the head Subj.[26]

Extending this analysis to *wh*-subject extraction in English, Rizzi and Shlonsky maintain that the same mechanism operates in English *wh*-subject interrogatives.

(112)   Who came?

In an earlier stage of this derivation, we have (113), where the *wh*-subject *who* is generated VP-internally and the Subj that is a head of the SubjP is merged with the structure.

(113)   Subj [... [who came]][27]

The interrogative subject *who* cannot be moved to the Spec-Subj; otherwise

---

[26] Although Rizzi and Shlonsky do not precisely outline a mechanism of realization of *qui*, it may be reasonable to say that the head Fin -*i* undergoes incorporation into or affixation onto C (*que*).

[27] Although they do not assign the label to the projection that is a sister of the head of the SubjP, it may be thought to be TP. See the structure in (102).

it would be stuck in that position under Criterial Freezing, and thus it could not be in the natural scope domain of a *wh*-operator.

(114) *[$_{SubjP}$ who [$_{Subj'}$ Subj [… [t_{who} came]]]]

Rizzi and Shlonsky (2007) further propose that English also has an option to make use of Fin, which is a counterpart of French Fin -*i* and consists of a full set of unvalued φ-features. Given this option, we have (115) instead of (114): Fin is merged with the SubjP to form FinP, to whose specifier the interrogative *who* moves, skipping the SubjP projection.

(115) [$_{FinP}$ who [$_{Fin'}$[$_{Fin}$ φ] [$_{SubjP}$ Subj [… [t_{who} came]]]]]

In (115) the Subject Criterion is satisfied by the head Fin with unvalued φ-features, which c-commands Subj, and the subject *wh*-interrogative values the (formerly) unvalued φ-features of Fin.

In the final stage of the derivation, Foc is merged with (115) to form a projection of Foc, to whose specifier the *wh*-subject moves and takes scope there.

(116) [$_{FocP}$ Who [$_{Foc'}$ Foc [$_{FinP}$ t$_{who}$ [$_{Fin'}$[$_{Fin}$ φ] [$_{SubjP}$ Subj [… [t_{who} came]]]]]]]

In this section, we have observed Rizzi and Shlonsky's (2007) Criterial Freezing approach to the subject. According to this approach, a subject of a sentence must meet the Subject Criterion, that is, a subject must be in a Spec-head configuration with its head. This analysis implies that the classical EPP, which states that all clauses must have a subject, can be reduced to the Subject Criterion. One prediction of the EPP, implied by the Subject Criterion, that holds in this situation is that a subject that moves to Spec-Subj from a VP-internal position is frozen in place. However, this prediction does not hold in one case, namely, in a *wh*-subject sentence, since a *wh*-subject must move to a scope position higher than SubjP. In order to solve this difficulty, Rizzi and Shlonsky propose Skipping Strategies: a *wh*-subject skips Spec-Subj and moves on to Spec-Foc, where it can take scope. In order to satisfy the Subject Criterion in such a case, they adopt the modified version of the criterion by Rizzi (2004) that is satisfied by the local head-head relation: thus, the head Subj must be c-commanded by Fin.

3.3.2. The Subject Criterion and Overt Complementizer-Copy Effects

In this subsection, we will examine how Rizzi and Shlonsky's analysis explains *for*- and *that*-copy effects, respectively demonstrated in (117) and

(118) below.

(117) *Who would you prefer [for [t_{who} Subj to win]]?[28]

(118) a. *Who did you say that t_{who} came?
      b. Who did you say t_{who} came?

Let us begin with (118b), where *that*-copy effects are obviated due to the absence of an overt complementizer. There are two potential ways to derive (118b). One option is demonstrated in (119), where the VP-internally generated subject is moved to Spec-Subj, satisfying the Subject Criterion. This derivation, however, cannot derive (118b), because the interrogative subject *who* is frozen in place in Spec-Subj and cannot move to a higher functional projection where it can take scope.

(119) *[$_{SubjP}$ who [$_{Subj'}$ Subj [$_{VP}$ t_{who} came]]]

The other option is to appeal to the skipping strategies in (106). In order to implement the strategies, Fin with unvalued φ-features has to be merged with SubjP, as represented in (120a), where the Subject Criterion is satisfied by Fin in a head-head relation with Subj, and the interrogative *wh*-subject moves to Spec-Fin, skipping Spec-Subj, as demonstrated in (120b).

(120) a. [$_{FinP}$ Fin[$_{SubjP}$ Subj [$_{VP}$ who came]]]
      b. [$_{FinP}$ who [$_{Fin'}$ Fin[$_{SubjP}$ Subj [$_{VP}$ t_{who} came]]]]

Unlike (119), the interrogative *who* here is not frozen in place, because it is not situated in Spec-Subj and thus can continue to move to a scope-taking position. Thus, (118b) can be derived.

A similar explanation can account for the ungrammaticality of (117). Rizzi and Shlonsky (2007) assume that the prepositional complementizer *for*, which does not have unvalued φ-features, lacks the ability to satisfy the Subject Criterion, which, in turn, means that the interrogative subject *who* must move to Spec-Subj, as demonstrated in (121):

(121) [$_{FinP}$ for [$_{SubjP}$ who [$_{Subj'}$Subj [to [$_{VP}$ t_{who}win]]]]]?

Once the interrogative subject *who* moves to Spec-Subj, it becomes frozen in place. Hence, (117) is ungrammatical.

Rizzi and Shlonsky's (2007) account of the ungrammaticality of (118a)

---

[28] Rizzi and Shlonsky do not account for the grammatical counterpart to (117):
  (i) Who would you prefer to win the race?

is slightly complicated. Based on the nature of the overt complementizer *that*, which expresses finiteness and (declarative) Force, they propose that the overt complementizer *that* generated in Fin undergoes head-movement to Force.

(122) [$_{ForceP}$ that [$_{FinP}$ t_{that} [$_{SubjP}$

According to them, *that* in (122) plays two roles simultaneously: that of a clausal argument, that is, the head of declarative (Force) that is selected by the main verb; and that of an expletive (Fin), satisfying the Subject Criterion.[29] They further argue that it is natural to assume that the same element cannot simultaneously function as an argument and an expletive. Note that even if a derivation of (118a) selects the skipping strategies, it is excluded by this assumption.

(123) *[$_{ForceP}$ who that [$_{FinP}$ t_{who} t_{that} [$_{SubjP}$ Subj [

Although in (123) the Subject Criterion is satisfied by Fin (t_{that}), (123 (=118a)) is excluded for the reason that the complementizer *that* functions as argument and expletive simultaneously.

3.3.3. Some Problems and Their Solutions

In the foregoing sections we have observed Rizzi and Shlonsky's (2007) analysis of overt and covert complementizer copy effects in terms of the Subject Criterion and the Freezing Effect. Their analysis is ingenious, but seems to have several problems.

The first such problem that comes to mind is the sentence structure that Rizzi and Shlonsky propose. According to them, there is a functional projection over TP, which they term the "Subject Phrase." The functional head "Subj" has a complete set of φ-features, and thereby, a VP-internally generated subject is attracted to Spec-Subj. This projection is strongly reminiscent of the functional projection "AgrP" proposed in the late GB era by Pollock (1989) and Belletti (1990) and maintained in early Minimalism. According to Belletti, AgrsP is projected above TP; thus, the D-structure and S-structure for a sentence are as in (124a) and (124b), respectively.

(124) a. [$_{AgrsP}$ [$_{Agrs'}$ Agrs [$_{TP}$ T [$_{AgroP}$ [$_{Agro'}$ Agro [$_{VP}$ Subj V Obj]]]]]]
      b. [$_{AgrsP}$ Subj [$_{Agrs'}$ Agrs [$_{TP}$ T [$_{AgroP}$ Obj [$_{Agro'}$ Agro [$_{VP}$ t_{Subj} V t_{Obj}]]]]]]

---

[29] Recall the argument regarding French *que-qui* alternation in 3.3.1, where *qui* was considered to consist of complementizer *que* and expletive *-i*, which belonged to Fin.

The subject and object are respectively attracted to Spec-Agrs and Spec-Agro for φ-feature checking.[30] This structure, in which the functional projection AgrPs seems to play a central role in predicting word order, can account for relative word order between a subject and an adverb or between an object and a verb.

However, Chomsky (1995) casts doubt on the existence of the category "Agr" on conceptual grounds: unlike other functional categories like T, C, and D, Agr does not have interpretable features and does not provide "instructions" at either or both interface levels (that is, PF and/or LF). Agr also has a peculiar property that other functional categories do not have: it disappears when it mediates agreement with a DP. As these facts imply, Agr exists only for theory-internal reason. Therefore, Chomsky (1995) abolishes the projection of Agr, assigning Agreement features to T and v*, and utilizing multiple specifiers.

(125) [$_{TP}$ Subj [$_{T'}$ T$_{[\varphi]}$ [$_{v*P(SPEC2)}$ Obj [$_{v*(SPEC1)}$ t$_{Subj}$ [$_{v*'}$ v*$_{[\varphi]}$ [$_{VP}$ V t$_{Obj}$]]]]]]

As shown in (125), φ-features are assigned to T and v* and the subject and the object move to Spec-T and (outer) Spec-v*, respectively; and the derived word order in (125) is the same as that in (124b). It can be concluded that there is no conceptual necessity for the existence of Agr.

The SubjP that Rizzi (2004) and Rizzi and Shlonsky (2007) propose can be seen to be analogous to the AgrsP that we have considered above in that the head Subj consists of a set of φ-features and drives movement of a subject generated VP internally. The functional head Agr is present only for agreement, and does not dedicate itself to "instructions" at interface levels. It follows from this that the postulation of Subj runs counter to the assumptions of Minimalism.

The postulation of the functional head Subj also leads to another problem for *wh*-subject extraction. In order to allow *wh*-subject extraction, as seen in (120), Rizzi and Shlonsky (2007) assume that a functional head Fin that has a full set of unvalued φ-features is merged to SubjP, and that Fin satisfies the Subject Criterion in the head-head agreement relation. If this is true, the functional head Subj must match Fin, which means they must have the same φ-features.

(126) [$_{FinP}$ Fin$_{[u\varphi]}$ [$_{SubjP}$ Subj$_{[\varphi]}$ [$_{vP}$ who$_{[\varphi]}$ [$_{v*}$ win]]]]

In (126) it is impossible for Fin$_{[u\varphi]}$ to agree with the *wh*-interrogative *who*

---

[30] Whether or not a subject or an object is attracted depends on feature strength.

due to the intervention of the functional head Subj$_{[\varphi]}$ (the defective intervention effect). Thus, the introduction of the functional head Subj causes conceptual problems.

However, it is possible in a more natural way to get the same effect that Rizzi and Shlonsky make an attempt to obtain without postulating a newly introduced functional head or a related criterion. We give (117) and (118) again as (127) and (128).

(127) *Who would you prefer [for [t_{who} to win]]?

(128) a. *Who did you say that t_{who} came?
      b. Who did you say t_{who} came?

Let us briefly observe how our analysis predicts the (un)grammaticality of (127) and (128).[31] Although (127) and (128a) have slightly different derivations, they are excluded in the same way, namely, by the RIC. The embedded CP of (127) is constructed by excorporation and subsequent merge of C-*for-to*, with the *wh*-subject raised from predicate-internal position to Spec-T, where the case [ACC] is assigned.

(129)   [$_{TP}$ /who$_{[ACC]}$/ [$_{T'}$ C-for$_{[ACC]}$ [$_{MP}$ ___ to [$_{v*P}$ {who} win]]]]

In the next stage of the derivation, the lexical complex C-*for* excorporates and merges with TP, to form a projection of C. Here, C has an uninterpretable focus feature [uF], which serves as a probe and locates *who*.

(130)   [$_{CP}$ C$_{[uF]}$-/for/ [$_{TP}$ [$_{DP}$ [F]who$_{[ACC]}$] [$_{T'}$ {for} [$_{MP}$ to [$_{v*P}$ {who} win]]]]]

However, C in (130) cannot attract *who* in Spec-T because the latter is inactive—in Rizzi and Shlonsky's term, frozen in place.

Let us now turn to (128a). In this case, the overt complementizer *that* does not constitute a lexical complex with T but instead is merged externally with a TP already built.

(131) a.   [$_{TP}$ /who$_{[NOM]}$/ [$_{T'}$ T$_{[NOM]}$ [$_{vP}$ {who} come]]]
      b.   [$_{CP}$ that$_{[uF]}$ [$_{TP}$ [F] /who$_{[NOM]}$/ [$_{T'}$ T$_{[NOM]}$ [$_{vP}$ {who} come]]]]

In (131b), the complementizer *that*, which has an uninterpretable focus feature [uF], serves as a probe and locates *who* in Spec-T. However, *that* can-

---

[31] The verb *prefer* can be thought of as belonging to the *want* class. See 3.2.3 for detailed discussion of derivation of sentences that contain this class of verb.

not attract *who*, because the *wh*-subject is inactive/frozen in place.

It is worth pointing out here that our Excorporation Analysis successfully derives that same effect as Rizzi and Shlonsky try to achieve *without* appealing to a newly introduced functional head.

Now let us turn to (128b). Here, the embedded CP is constructed by excorporation and subsequent merge of the lexical complex C-T, with the predicate-internal subject attracted for case-theoretic reasons.

(132) [$_{CP/TP}$[F] /who$_{[NOM]}$/ [C$_{[uF]}$-T$_{[NOM]}$ [$_{vP}$ {who} came]]]

In (132), the uninterpretable features are all checked, and thus excorporation and merge of the lexical complex C-T do not occur. This means that the categorial status of the topmost projection is CP as well as TP. When the matrix v*P is constructed, the phase head v* can attract *who* into its specifier position because it is the head of an A-bar chain, not an A-chain, as seen from the matrix phase head v*. Remember that the RIC is sensitive to the head of the A-chain. Thus, to sum up, in contrast with Rizzi and Shlonsky's analysis, our analysis is free from such dubious functional heads as "Fin" and "Subj."

Chapter 4

Extraction from Objects

Much of the discussion in the previous chapters has centered on the analysis of total extraction and subextraction of a *wh*-phrase from a subject in terms of the excorporation. In this chapter, we will discuss how our analysis, which is based on the Revised Inactivity Condition (RIC), predicts *wh*-extraction from an object.

4.1. Extraction from Objects and Its Problems

In the previous chapters, we have seen how the Excorporation Analysis coupled with the RIC explains the (un)grammaticality of extraction from a subject. Some of the data that have been discussed have included the following.

(1) a. Of which major is it important for the students to take a course in physics?
 b. *Who is it important for to take a course in physics?

Although it has been shown that the RIC plays a crucial role in predicting the (un)grammaticality of (1), some doubt seems to be cast on our analysis by the grammaticality of extraction from the object, demonstrated in (2).

(2) Who will you see?

In order to allay the doubt that (2) casts on our analysis, it may be helpful at this point to briefly review how our analysis predicts the (un)grammaticality of (1) above. Let us begin with the final stage of the derivation of the embedded v*P phase, which is built by excorporation and subsequent merge of v*-/*take*/ with the VP already built, as well as the external argument generated in Spec-v*.

(3)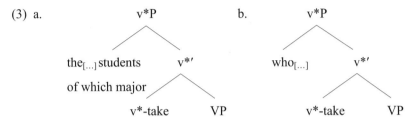

A lexical complex C-T(*for*)-M(*to*) is merged with v*P to form an MP, followed by excorporation and merge of the lexical complex C-*for* with the MP, forming a TP. Remember that *for* has case feature [ACC], and that the D of the external arguments also has an unvalued case feature […].[1]

(4)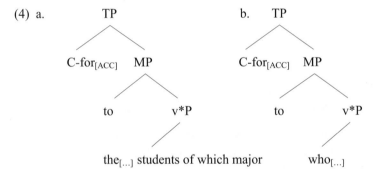

We assume that in English case is assigned to the DP under Merge to a case-assigning category. Thus, the external argument undergoes Internal Merge (IM) to TP, and the unvalued case is valued as [ACC].

---

[1] We leave out the φ-features of *for* and the subject.

Chapter 4 Extraction from Objects   119

(5)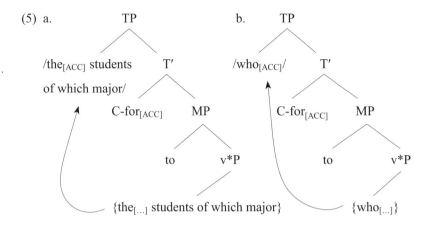

In the next stage of the derivation, the lexical complex C-/for/ excorporates and merges with TP, forming a projection of C.

(6)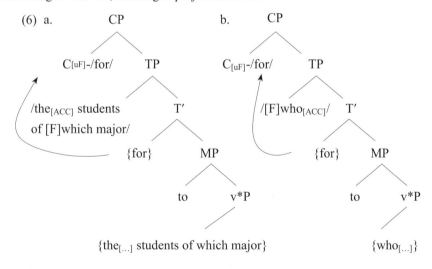

As discussed in 2.3.3, we assume with Tonoike (2000) that an interrogative C has an uninterpretable focus feature [uF], which serves as a probe and locates a *wh*-phrase, and further that an interpretable counterpart [F] is generated in the Spec-D of a *wh*-phrase. In (6), the C with [uF] finds as its goal two *wh*-phrases that are both in Spec-v* and in Spec-T. IM of the *wh*-phrase from Spec-v* to Spec-C is impossible in both these cases, because the copy left behind in v*P consists of semantic features but not phonological features. In our analysis, IM of elements with no phonetic shapes is prohibited by the Overt Syntax Hypothesis of Tonoike (2008a), which states that IM must carry an element with a phonetic shape. It then follows that the goal of the [uF] of C is the *wh*-phrase in Spec-T. While IM of a *wh*-phrase from Spec-T in (6a) is possible, it is impossible from Spec-T in (6b). This fact can be made to follow from the RIC proposed in Chapter 2, which is repeated below as (7).

(7) Revised Inactivity Condition (RIC)
D and N that head the head of an A-chain become invisible to further computation when their uninterpretable features are valued.

In the external argument of (6a), the invisible element is the D, because the uninterpretable feature, which is the case feature [ACC], is valued, and thus the rest of the elements are visible to further computation. Therefore, it is possible to extract a *wh*-phrase *of which major*. However, the external argument of (6b) *who*, whose categorial status is D, is assigned case and becomes invisible to further computation, and the RIC bans the *wh*-phrase from being extracted.

Our analysis, which is crucially dependent on the RIC, makes one prediction: subextraction of a *wh*-phrase should always be possible, even if a phrase containing a *wh*-phrase is case-assigned, but total extraction of a *wh*-phrase which itself is case-assigned should always be impossible. However, this prediction is not borne out: *wh*-extraction from the object of a transitive verb is always possible, whether or not extraction is total.

(8) a. Who will you see?
    b. Of which car did you find a picture?

The same holds true for *wh*-extraction from a prepositional complement position.

(9) Which city will you live in?

Although the complement of a preposition is always case-assigned, total extraction of a *wh*-phrase is nevertheless always possible.

In pre-Minimalist approaches, the ECP (Empty Category Principle) captures in a natural way the fact that extraction is easier from an object of a transitive verb or prepositions, since their object positions are always properly governed by the transitive verb or the preposition.[2] It goes without saying, however, that we cannot resort to the ECP in the Minimalist Program,

---

[2] For the definition and discussion of proper government, see Chapter 3.

because the notion of (proper) government, on which the ECP is defined, is dispensed with.

There seem to be several potential ways to make it possible for a *wh*-object to be extracted without violating the RIC. One possibility is to assume that *wh*-extraction from a complement position of a verb or a preposition is insensitive to the RIC. This assumption, however, cannot be maintained from a theoretical point of view, because we assume that the RIC strictly constrains the IM (Move) operation. Assuming that the RIC does not apply to an object *wh*-phrase, the RIC, which we crucially rely on, will lose its force.

Another possibility is to resort to certain aspects of the nature of the A-chain. As is assumed by Chomsky (1986b), there are two kinds of A-chain: nontrivial and trivial. The former chains are constituted by the A-movement operation and thus the chain is made up of more than one member of chain, a head and a tail. The latter chains are yielded by the External Merge of an argument to a θ-position. It then follows that an object *wh*-phrase constitutes a trivial chain when merged to the complement of the main verb. It may be possible to extract a case-assigned object *wh*-phrase by assuming that the RIC is insensitive to (the head of) a trivial chain. However, it seems stipulative to distinguish non-trivial chains from trivial ones. Thus, we will not resort to this argument from the nature of A-chain.

Another possibility is to adopt the assumption that an object *wh*-phrase simultaneously undergoes A-movement for case-assignment and A-bar-movement by v*'s [EF], in the sense of Chomsky (2008). In order to see how this assumption interacts with the RIC, we need to review the analysis of a *wh*-object by Chomsky (2008). Let us examine how (2), which is repeated as (10) below, is derived.

(10) Who will you see?

In the v*P phase, the main verb V (*see*) inherits from v* unvalued φ-features and the case feature [ACC]. The unvalued φ-features then are valued by the agreement holding between the V and the object. The *wh*-object *who*, which has an unvalued case feature [...], moves to Spec-V, where the accusative case is assigned by the main verb *see*, which inherits the case feature [ACC] from v*. Notice here that v* has the feature [EF] as well as φ-features and a case feature: this [EF] serves as a probe and locates a *wh*-phrase. In the case of (10) there are two possible *wh*-phrases for attraction by [EF]: one in Spec-V and one in the complement of the main verb. However, it is impossible to attract the *wh*-phrase in Spec-V, which is the head of an A-chain and whose uninterpretable feature, the unvalued case feature, is valued. Attraction of such an element would violate the Inactivity Condition. It then follows that the *wh*-movement takes place from the complement position of the main verb *see*. The *wh*-phrase in the complement of the main verb is not the head of an A-chain, and its unvalued feature is not valued, which means that it can be attracted without violating the Inactivity Condition. We should note here that the A-movement and A-bar-movement of the *wh*-phrase takes place simultaneously in the v*P phase.

(11)

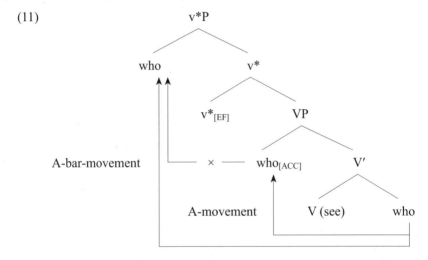

It is true that this analysis makes it possible for an object *wh*-phrase to be attracted without violating the Inactivity Condition, but it also creates some new complications of its own. One such complication concerns the newly introduced "feature inheritance" operation. The motivation for this operation can be found in the assumption that all movement operations, be they A-movement or A-bar movement, are driven by phase heads, that is, v* and C. Features that drive movement of the subject and the object must be inherited by T and V, respectively, for the subject and the object to be able to move to Spec-T and Spec-V (respectively). While these movement operations are integrated into the phase heads (v* and C), a new operation, namely inheritance, is introduced, which complicates UG.

Furthermore, A-movement of the object *wh*-phrase and head-movement of the main verb (*see*) to v* violates the Extension Condition, which requires that a Merge operation extend the structure. Thus, though it may seem initially appealing to adopt the A- and A-bar movement analysis of a *wh*-

phrase, it is difficult to adopt such a simultaneous movement analysis due to complications that it creates.

Alternatively, one may argue that it is possible to transplant a simultaneous A- and A-bar movement analysis into an Excorporation Analysis, claiming that the main verb is inherently the case-assigner and that the object *wh*-phrase is attracted to Spec-V, leaving a copy in the complement position of the main verb, followed by excorporation of the lexical complex v*-V.

(12)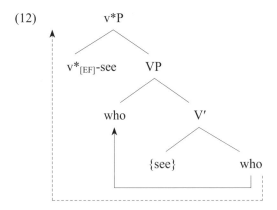

The [EF] feature of v* attracts a *wh*-phrase in the complement of the main verb, as discussed by Chomsky (2008). This analysis seems attractive, but we cannot adopt it because we crucially depend on assumption (13) for case-assignment in English.

(13) In English case is assigned under Merge to the case-assigning category.

In our analysis, an object *wh*-phrase is assigned accusative case when it is merged with a main verb that has case feature [ACC]. As for the empirical consequences of (13), see 2.3.1 for details.

In this section, we have examined some possible analyses and seen that each has its own problems. However, there remains another way of dealing with extraction of an object *wh*-phrase, which I believe is the most promising. In the next section, we will explore this possibility.

4.2. A Solution

The goal of this section is to show that although the RIC constrains *wh*-

extraction from the object of a transitive verb or a preposition, a *wh*-phrase can nevertheless be extracted successfully without incurring violation of the RIC.

4.2.1. Simultaneous Syntactic Relation and the RIC

Before delving into this issue, we shall review the proposed analysis by Egashira and Tonoike (2010, 2012), which enables *wh*-movement from objects of transitive verbs and prepositions to be implemented without violating the Inactivity Condition.

As argued above, assuming that a *wh*-phrase is case-assigned when merged with a transitive verb or a preposition, *wh*-movement from the object position of a transitive verb or a preposition violates the Revised Inactivity Condition (RIC), and as a result (14), would be excluded—wrongly, given its grammaticality.

(14) a. Who do you see?
b. Which city do you live in?

Given this state of affairs, Egashira and Tonoike argue that the simultaneous syntactic operations driven by the lexical complex v*-V allow an object *wh*-phrase to be extracted successfully. Let us begin with (14a). In an early stage of its derivation, we have (15), where a lexical complex v*-V (*see*) is merged with *what* to form a VP.

(15)

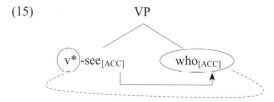

When the lexical complex v*-V (*see*) and the complement are merged, the unvalued case feature [...] of the complement *who* has is valued in accordance with case-assignment in (13) above.[3] At the same time, an agreement relation holds between v* and *what*. We consider this agreement to involve identification of a *wh*-phrase by v*, and assume that a phase head v* identifies a *wh*-phrase as a target of Internal Merge (or attraction) to its Spec. The dotted line in (15) shows this identification relation. We assume

---

[3] We leave out the φ-feature agreement holding between the main verb and its complement.

that once this identification holds, it continues to hold throughout the derivation in the v*P phase. In the next stage of the derivation, v* excorporates and merges with the VP to form v*P, to whose specifier an external argument *you* is merged.

(16)

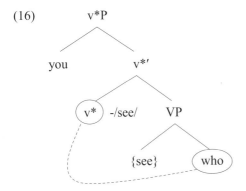

The phase head v* serves as a probe and locates *what* in the VP, attracting it to the outer Spec-v*.

(17)

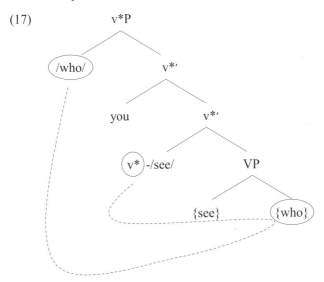

It might be objected that the *wh*-movement in (17) violates the RIC because the *wh*-phrase has already been assigned [ACC] in the VP before being attracted to Spec-v*. However, as seen in (15), the probes V (*see*) and v* locate *who* simultaneously. We assume that this simultaneous syntactic operation makes it possible for a *wh*-phrase to be extracted even if it is the inactive head of an A-chain.

Similar considerations hold in contexts of preposition-stranding, as seen in (14b), repeated here as (18).

(18)   Which city do you live [_PP_ in ___]?

In (18), the *wh*-phrase has been case-assigned in the complement of the preposition, which is a case-assigning category. The RIC would prohibit *wh*-movement from being applied to (18); however, Egashira and Tonoike argue that this can be avoided by resort to the Excorporation Analysis, coupled with the assumption that the simultaneous agreement relation holding between v* and a preposition deactivates the RIC. In the case of (18), the main verb *live* and the preposition *in* constitute an idiom that means 'inhabit.' Based on this fact, Egashira and Tonoike assume (19):

(19)   A preposition can be a part of the lexical complex of v*-V if the preposition and verb form an idiom together.

Given (19), in an earlier stage of the derivation of (18) we will have (20), where the preposition *in* is a part of the lexical complex v*-*live-in*, taking the *wh*-phrase *which city* as its complement. Notice that the preposition and *wh*-phrase respectively have case feature [OBL(ique)] and unvalued case feature [...].[4]

(20)

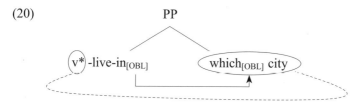

In (20), *in* and v* serve as a probe and simultaneously locate *which city*. The unvalued case feature of the *wh*-phrase is valued in accordance with the assumption concerning case-assignment in (13), which states that in English case is assigned under Merge to the case-assigning category. At the same time, v* identifies the object *wh*-phrase under the agreement holding between v* and *which city*, shown with the dotted line in (20) above.

---

[4] We implicitly assume that a preposition also has unvalued φ-features to be valued by the complement DP. We leave further investigation of the relation in (20) for future research.

Chapter 4 Extraction from Objects 127

In the next stage of the derivation, v*-*live* excorporates and merges with the PP to form a VP, as in (21) below.

(21)

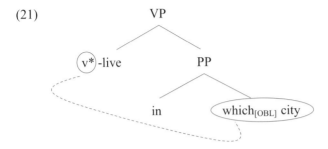

The *wh*-phrase in (16) has not yet been attracted, presumably because Spec-V is not a possible landing site for a *wh*-phrase. Note, however, that the identification relation holding between v* and the *wh*-phrase is maintained.

In the next stage of the derivation, v* excorporates and merges with the VP to form v*P, to whose specifier position the external argument *they* is merged.

(22)

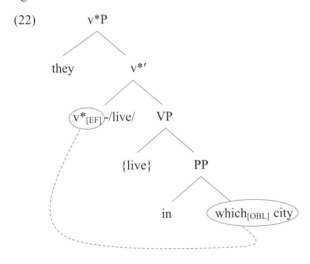

In (22), the identification relation holding between v* and the *wh*-phrase is still maintained, as shown by the dotted line. The phase head v*, which has the feature [EF], serves as a probe and locates the *wh*-phrase in the complement of preposition *in*. The *wh*-phrase undergoes attraction to Spec-v*, as shown in (23) below.

(23)

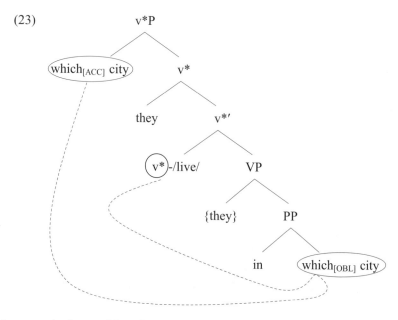

As argued above, this *wh*-movement does not violate the RIC because in an earlier stage of derivation, v* and P enter simultaneous syntactic relation with the *wh*-phrase: simultaneously, P assigns oblique case to, and v* identifies, the *wh*-phrase.

In this subsection, we have examined Egashira and Tonoike's proposal concerning successful extraction of an object *wh*-phrase without violating RIC. However, there seems to remain a question of why the simultaneous syntactic relation deactivates RIC. We will discuss this issue in the next subsection.

4.2.2. The Nature of the Simultaneous Syntactic Relation

Although it is true that the simultaneous syntactic relations holding between a phase head v* and a *wh*-phrase on the one hand and a case-assigning category and a *wh*-phrase on the other circumvent the violation of the RIC, the question arises of why this syntactic relation plays a crucial role in enabling a *wh*-phrase to move without incurring violation of the RIC. In Chapter 3, we observed a case where a *wh*-phrase could be successfully extracted from the case-assigned position without violating the RIC. If we can attribute the specific nature of the simultaneous syntactic relation observed in *wh*-extraction from the complement of a transitive verb and a preposition to whatever permits *wh*-extraction from a case-assigned subject position, we can explain case-assigned *wh*-extraction from both subject and object positions in a unified way, maintaining the RIC.

Let us consider again the phenomenon that permits *wh*-extraction from a case-assigned position without violating the RIC. The outline font in (24) below indicates a copy.

(24) Who do you think [who will see Mary]

In (24), a nominative-assigned *wh*-phrase is extracted successfully, without incurring violation of the RIC. Let us review how our Excorporation Analysis derives (24). The embedded v*P is built by excorporation and subsequent merge of a lexical complex v*-*see*, and merge of the external argument *who* with the projection of v*.

(25)

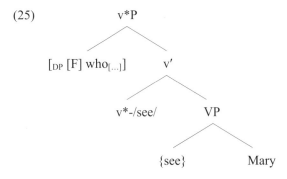

We assume that the *wh*-subject in (25) has unvalued case feature [...] and interpretable focus feature [F] in Spec-D. In the next stage of the derivation, C-T-M (*will*) is merged to v*P to form an MP, followed by excorporation and subsequent merge of C-T-/will/ to the MP respectively.[5] C and T in (26) below carry the features [uF] and [NOM], respectively.

---

[5] In (26), the VP undergoes the transfer operation.

(26)

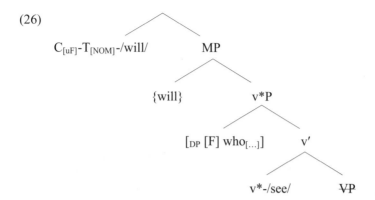

In the next stage of the derivation, the subject *who* in Spec-v* is raised, for case-theoretic reasons.

(27)

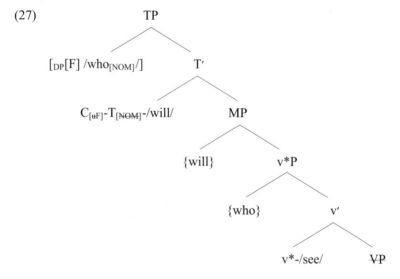

In (27), the unvalued case feature [...] of the subject is valued, and the case feature [NOM] of T is checked and deleted. We should recall that the uninterpretable [uF] of C can be checked by its interpretable counterpart of the subject in (27). Thus, there are no uninterpretable features in the lexical complex C-T-/*will*/, and as a result there is no further excorporation or subsequent merge of the lexical complex. This means that the topmost projection is not only TP but also CP.

Chapter 4 Extraction from Objects   131

(28)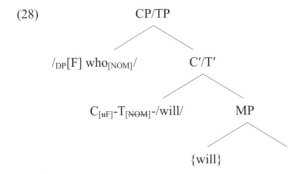

In the matrix v*P phase, the lexical complex v*-*think* is merged to (28) to form a VP, followed by excorporation and subsequent merge of the lexical complex, forming a projection of v*, with which the external argument is merged.

(29)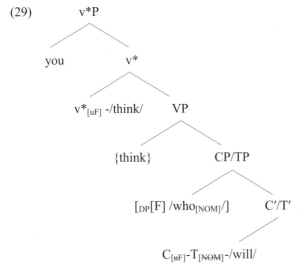

Seen from the embedded T part of the C$_{[uF]}$-T$_{[NOM]}$-/*will*/, the categorial status of the projection of the embedded clause is TP; however, seen from the matrix V {*think*}, it is CP. Matrix phase head v* has uninterpretable focus feature [uF] to be checked and deleted. Hence, the v* serves as a probe and locates a *wh*-subject in the embedded clause, attracting it to its specifier position. This attraction seems to violate the RIC. However, seen from v*, the position of the *wh*-subject is Spec-C, not Spec-T, which means that the *wh*-subject occupies an A-bar-position, not an A-position and further that it heads an A-bar chain, not an A-chain. This in turn means that IM (movement) of *who* to the matrix Spec-v* can be implemented without incurring violation of the RIC, which is sensitive to the head of an A-chain. In this way, the analysis of the dual categorial status of the projection makes it possible for a case-assigned *wh*-phrase to be extracted without violating the RIC.

Now let go back to the case of *wh*-extraction from the complement of a transitive verb or a preposition.

(30) a. What did you find?
b. Which city do you live in?

As pointed out, in an early stage of the derivation, both sentences have the following configuration.

(31) a.   VP   b.   PP

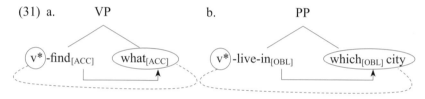

The point here is that the case-assigning categories *find* and *in* and the phase head v* that drives A-bar movement all "see" its complement *what* and *which city* at the same time, respectively. It is then possible to analyze that seen from a case-assigning category, in which case its complement position is A-position, whereas seen from the position of phase head v*, the complement of the V and P in (31) is A'-position. The syntactic status of the position occupied by a *wh*-phrase observed in (31) is strongly reminiscent of that of the position occupied by a subject *wh*-phrase observed in (29) above. In (29), the position occupied by a subject *wh*-phrase *who* is both an A-position and an A-bar-position at the same time, whereas seen from the perspective of the matrix phase head v*, it is an A-bar-position. If this reasoning is correct, it can be concluded that the *wh*-phrase in object position is considered to be in A-bar position when attracted by v* to its outer Spec, which in turn means that there is no violation of the RIC, because the RIC is sensitive to the head of an A-chain, not that of an A-bar chain.

4.3. Extraction from Subjects of ECM

In 4.2.2, we have observed that the position occupied by an argument *wh*-phrase has dual syntactic status: it is an A-position when seen from a case-assigning category such as V or P, and an A-bar position when seen from a phase head. This analysis can also account for the grammaticality of *wh*-extraction of a subject of an Exceptional Case Marking (ECM) construction.

(32) Who do you expect to win the race?

Now let us see how our Excorporation Analysis derives such an ECM construction as that in (33) below.[6]

(33) I expect him to win the race.

We assume here that the matrix v* constitutes a lexical complex with the main verb and the infinitive, v*-V-M. Suppose, however, that this lexical complex merges with the embedded v*P to form an MP. (Recall that infinitival *to* belongs to the category M(odal)).[7]

(34)

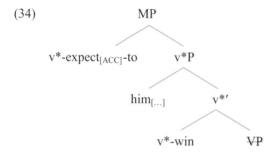

In the next stage of the derivation, the lexical complex excorporates and merges with the MP, to form a projection of the V. The ECM subject, which has unvalued case feature [...], is merged (raised) to the category that has valued case feature [ACC], namely, to Spec-V, as seen in (35) below.[8, 9]

---

[6] Strictly, we should use the term "object-raising construction," not "ECM construction." However, for ease of exposition, we will retain the term with "ECM."

[7] We assume that the embedded VP is transferred.

[8] In contrast with Chomsky's (2008) analysis of the ECM construction, we find a MP between the main verb projection and the embedded v*P. As a result, the ECM subject undergoes raising in one fell swoop to Spec-V.

[9] Our analysis can also capture the phenomena pointed out by Postal (1974) and Lasnik and Saito (1992), because the ECM subject undergoes overt movement to Spec-V. (See 1.2.6 and 3.2.4 for details on those arguments.)

(35)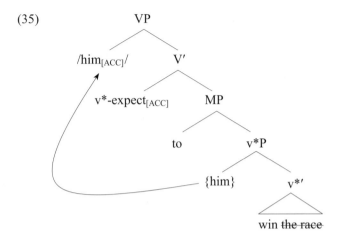

The lexical complex v*-*expect* excorporates and merges with VP to form the projection v*, with which the external argument is merged. As argued throughout this book, the external argument *I* has unvalued case feature [...].

(36)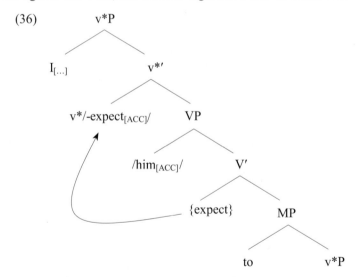

In the matrix CP phase, the lexical complex C-T is merged to (36) forming a projection of T, which has the case feature [NOM]. The external argument is raised to Spec-T for case-theoretic reasons, as seen in (37) below.[10]

---

[10] In (37) VP undergoes the Transfer operation. The C-T complex will not excorporate and merge to TP, because there are no uninterpretable features to force such an operation.

(37)

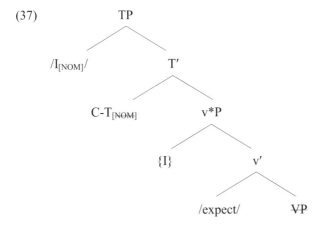

With this derivation in mind, let us now go back to (32). In the embedded MP, we have (38), where the lexical complex v*-*expect-to* is merged with v*P to form the MP. Recall that the ECM subject *wh*-phrase *who* has an interpretable focus feature [F] in its Spec, as well as an unvalued case feature [...], and that the matrix phase head v* has an uninterpretable focus feature [uF].

(38)

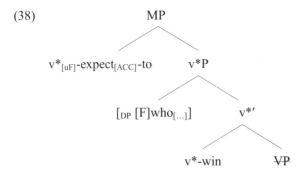

In the next stage of the derivation, v*$_{[uF]}$-*expect* excorporates and merges with the MP to form a VP.

(39)

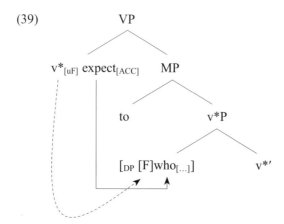

In the stage of the derivation shown in (39), v* and the main verb *expect* "see" the *wh*-ECM subject at the same time. The ECM subject is raised to Spec-V for case-theoretic reasons, as demonstrated in (40).

(40)

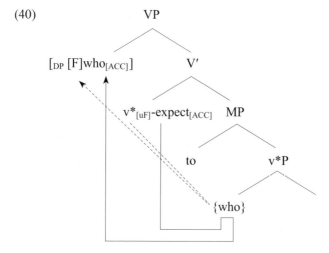

We assume that the syntactic relation that holds in an earlier stage of the derivation will continue to hold at a later stage. Specifically, in the case that we are dealing with, the syntactic relation that holds in (39) still holds in (40). In (40), the phase head $v^*_{[uF]}$ and the main verb *expect* "see" the ECM subject in Spec-V. In the next stage of the derivation, v* excorporates and merges with the VP, maintaining the syntactic relation from (39) to (40).

Chapter 4 Extraction from Objects 137

(41)

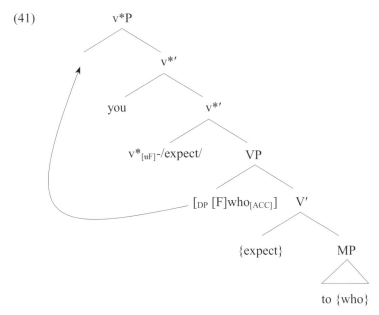

In the following stage of the derivation, the ECM verb v*-/*expect*/ with an uninterpretable focus feature [uF] raises the ECM subject *who* from Spec-V into Spec-v*. This movement appears to violate the RIC, because the ECM subject *who* that is case-assigned in Spec-V is the head of an A-chain. However, as argued above, the syntactic relation that held in an earlier stage of the derivation still holds in the present stage: in (41), seen from the v* part of the lexical complex v*-/*expect*/, the ECM subject *who* is considered to be in an A-bar-position, not in an A-position. In other words, the ECM subject *who* in (41) heads a trivial A-bar chain, which means that *wh*-extraction can be successfully implemented without violating the RIC.

In the matrix CP phase, after excorporation and subsequent merge of the lexical complex C-T-M (*do*), A-movement of the matrix subject takes place from Spec-v* to Spec-T, and A-bar-movement of the interrogative ECM subject takes place to the matrix Spec-C.

(42) [$_{CP}$ /Who$_{[F]}$/ [$_{C'}$ C$_{[uF]}$-T-/do/ [$_{TP}$ /you/ [$_{MP}$ [$_{v*P}$ {who} [$_{v*}$ v*-/*expect*/

As final remarks on this section, let us consider the subextraction of a *wh*-phrase from an ECM subject, as seen in (43) below.

(43) Of which car do you expect the driver to avoid an accident?[11]

In (43) the *wh*-phrase *of which car* is subextracted from the ECM subject.

Chomsky's argument regarding this subextraction is as follows. In the matrix v*P phase, the ECM subject is raised to Spec-V from Spec-T for case-theoretic reasons.[12]

(44)

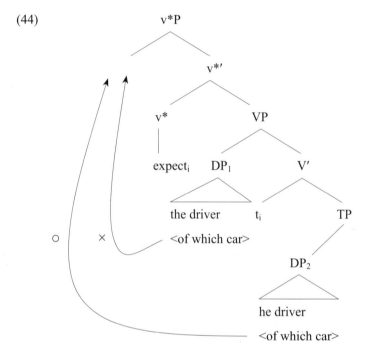

Chomsky argues that *wh*-extraction here is implemented at the same time as movement of the ECM subject. There are two copies of the ECM subject, which contains a *wh*-phrase; this means that there are also two possible *wh*-phrases that will be attracted by a phase head v*: one in DP_1 and the other in DP_2. The attraction of the former is excluded by Chomsky's Inactivity Condition, because DP_1, which is the head of an A-chain, has no unvalued features. The attraction of the latter does not violate the Inactivity Condi-

---

[11] I have simplified Chomsky's (2008) example, which contains subextraction of a *wh*-phrase from the ECM subject. The full example by Chomsky is as follows.
(i) of which car did they believe the (driver, picture) to have caused a scandal
(Chomsky (2008: 153))

[12] As to the derivation of ECM by Chomsky, see 1.2.6 for details.

tion, since the case feature of DP_2 is not valued.

Now let us see how our Excorporation Analysis deals with (43). Suppose that the derivation of (43) proceeds to (45), where the ECM subject *the driver of which car* is raised to Spec-V for case-theoretic reasons.

(45)
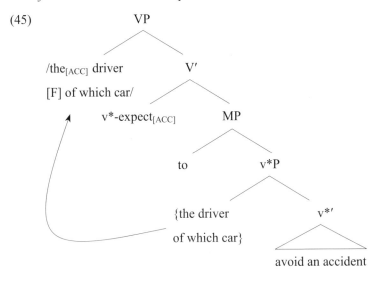

In the next stage of the derivation, the lexical complex v*-*expect* excorporates and merges with the VP, to form a projection of v*, with which the matrix subject is merged.

(46)
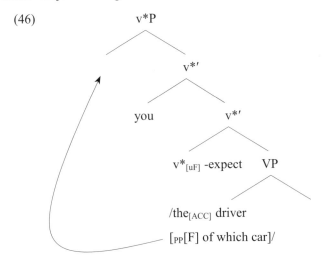

The uninterpretable focus feature [uF] is assigned to v*, which serves as a probe and locates the PP in the ECM subject. The *wh*-phrase PP *of which car* is raised to Spec-v*. Notice here that the *wh*-movement does not violate the RIC, which states that the D and N are frozen in place when assigned case. Even if the IC, not the RIC, is adopted, the *wh*-phrase can still be successfully extracted, because, as argued from (39) to (41), seen from the main verb *expect* of the lexical complex, Spec-V is an A-position whereas seen from the v* of the lexical complex, Spec-v* is an A'-position, and the (R) IC is sensitive to a DP in A-position.

4.4. Extraction from Subjects of Other Types of Object-Raising Constructions

In the previous section, we have observed how our Excorporation Analysis derives ECM constructions, and further, how it derives total extraction and subextraction of a *wh*-phrase from the ECM subject. This complementary subsection examines total and subextraction from subjects of other constructions that seem to involve object-raising, namely, Acc(usative)-*ing* gerunds and constructions that involve a perceptual verb or causative verb.

4.4.1. Extraction from a Subject of an Acc-*ing* Gerund

In this subsection we focus on gerunds containing an accusative subject, shown in (47) below.

(47) I remember him having avoided an accident.

Nakajima (1991) persuasively argues that this Acc-*ing* consists of a TP, indicating that Acc-*ing* behaves in a similar way to ECM complements. The most interesting and relevant data from his analysis for our discussion is as follows.

(48) a. John considers [Mary *probably* to be scared of snakes]
         — certainly, she is scared of snakes.   (Nakajima (1991: 40))
     b. I remember John certainly having agreed.   (Ibid.: 42)

In (48a), the adverb *probably*, which modifies the matrix verb *considers*, appears in the ECM complement. As shown in (48b), the adverb *certainly* distributes in the same way as (48a): it appears in the clausal gerund (i.e., in the form Acc-*ing*). On the basis of this distributional fact regarding the adverbs in (48), Nakajima argues that the categorial status of Acc-*ing* is the same as that of the ECM complement, that is, TP. The distribution of the adverbs in (48) not only shows a similarity of categorial status between Acc-*ing* and the ECM complement, but also that the subject of Acc-*ing* undergoes raising to the matrix clause, out of TP. As argued in 1.2.6 and 4.3, the ECM subject is raised to the matrix clause; in (48a) the subject of the ECM complement *Mary* moves out of the ECM complement over the adverb *probably*, which modifies the matrix verb *considers*.

(49) John considers Mary$_i$ probably [t_i to be scared of snakes]

Although in (48b) the adverb *certainly* modifying the matrix verb *remember* appears to occur unnaturally within Acc-*ing*, we can explain the relative distribution of the adverb and the subject of Acc-*ing John* in a more natural way if the subject is assumed to move out of the clausal gerund, as shown in (50) below.

(50) I remember John$_i$ certainly [t_i having agreed].

The order of the subject of Acc-*ing* and the adverb relative to one another seems to suggest that the subject undergoes raising to the matrix clause.

Binding phenomena also suggest that a subject of Acc-*ing* undergoes raising to the matrix clause. Let us observe (51) below.

(51) a. *John believes him$_i$ to be a genius [even more fervently than Bob$_i$ does].
  b. The DA proved the defendants$_i$ to be guilty [during each other's$_i$ trials].   (Lasnik and Saito (1991))

(51a) is ungrammatical in the interpretation where *him* corefers with *Bob*, while (51b) is grammatical in the interpretation where *defendants* corefers with *each other*. This suggests that (51a) and (51b) violate and observe Binding Condition C and A, respectively. These facts suggest that ECM subjects are raised higher than adjunct phrases adjoined to a matrix VP. With this in mind, observe (52).

(52) a. *John remembered him$_i$ being a genius even more clearly than Bob$_i$ did.
  b. The DA remembered the two men$_i$ very clearly being guilty during each other's$_i$ trials.

The same phenomena that we observed in (51) above can also be observed in (52). Specifically, (52a) is ungrammatical in the interpretation in which *him*, which is the subject of Acc-*ing*, corefers with *Bob*, while (52b) is grammatical in the interpretation in which *the two men* is the antecedent of *each other*. These facts indicate that (52a) and (52b) respectively violate and observe Binding Condition C and A, respectively. This in turn means that the subject of Acc-*ing* in (52) is raised higher than the adjunct phrases, as is the subject of an ECM complement.

Another piece of evidence lending support to the claim that the subject of Acc-*ing* is raised to the matrix clause can be found in the licensing of Negative Polarity Items (NPIs). Observe (53).

(53) a. **Anybody* didn't come.
b. Mary didn't see *anyone*. (Laka (1990: 21))

While in (53a) an NPI *anybody* appears in the subject position and the grammaticality of (53a) is degraded, in (53b) an NPI *anyone* appears in the object position and the grammaticality of (53b) is not degraded. In other words, in (53a) the NPI is not c-commanded by the negative element (*n't*), but in (53b) it is. This leads Laka (1990) to propose that NPIs must be c-commanded by a negative element in overt syntax.[13] With this property of NPIs in mind, now let us observe (54).

(54) The DA remembered none of the defendants being guilty during *any* of the trials.

In (54), an NPI *any* is included in an adjunct phrase adjoined to the matrix VP. The grammaticality of (54) suggests that the NPI *any* is c-commanded by the negative element *none*. This means that the subject of Acc-*ing* is raised higher than the adjunct phrase.

(55) The DA remembered *none of the defendants*ᵢ [tᵢ being guilty [during any of the trials]]

We can safely conclude from the discussion above that the subject of Acc-*ing*, like that of an ECM complement, is raised out of a clausal gerund. We assume that it is raised to the matrix Spec-V, for case-theoretic reasons. Thus, we assume that Acc-*ing* gerunds have the same structure and derivation as ECM constructions.

Taking (55) as an example, let us examine how the Acc-*ing* is de-

---

[13] Laka (1990) proposes in the framework of Government and Binding Theory that Negative Polarity Items must be c-commanded by a negative element in the S-structure.

rived. In the earlier stage of the derivation, we have (56).

(56)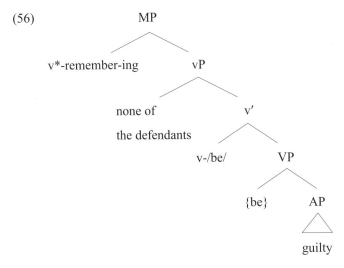

We assume here that the gerundive affix *-ing* constitutes a lexical complex with v*-*remember*, which is itself a lexical complex, and that the gerundive affix belongs to M.[14] In (56), the lexical complex v*-*remember-ing* is merged with vP, forming MP.

In the next stage of the derivation, the matrix verb *remember* excorporates and is merged with the MP to form a VP, to which we assume that the adjunct PP is adjoined.

---

[14] Given the minimal pair in (i) below, it is natural to assume that the gerundive *-ing* in the Acc-*ing* construction belongs to the Modal.
    (i) a. I remember to post the letter.
        b. I remember posting the letter.
The infinitival *to* in (a) can be assumed to be M. See 4.3 for details.

(57)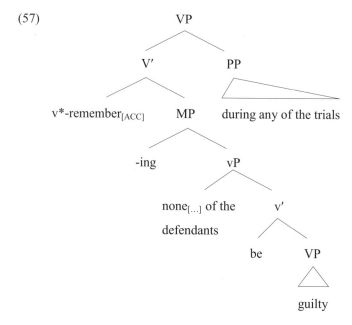

Notice here that the matrix verb *remember* has an accusative case feature [ACC], while the subject of Acc-*ing* has an unvalued case feature [...]. As a result, in the next stage of the derivation, the embedded subject is raised to the Spec-V, where its unvalued case is valued as [ACC], and v* excorporates and merges with the VP, pied-piping the sound of the main verb *remember* and projecting v*P, to whose specifier position the matrix subject is merged.

Chapter 4 Extraction from Objects 145

(58)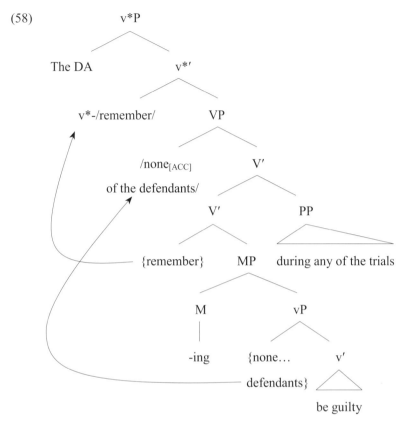

In (58), the raised subject *none of the defendants* c-commands the NPI *any*, satisfying the license condition of the NPI.

In the final derivation, a lexical complex C-T is merged to v*P, with the matrix subject *the DA* raised to Spec-T for case-theoretic reasons.

(59) [$_{CP/TP}$/The DA$_{[NOM]}$/[$_{T'}$ C-T$_{[NOM]}$[$_{v*P}$ {the DA} [$_{v*'}$ v*-remembered [$_{VP}$]]]]^{15}

We have observed that Acc-*ing* gerunds are derived in the same way as ECM constructions: a subject of Acc-*ing* undergoes raising to the matrix Spec-V. If this analysis is on the right track, one prediction will hold that total extraction of and subextraction from the subject of Acc-*ing* is possible; and this prediction is indeed borne out, as seen in (60) below.

---

[15] In (59), the categorial status of the topmost projection is not only TP but also CP.

(60) a. Who do you remember causing an accident?
b. Of which car do you remember the driver causing an accident?[16]

Let us see how our analysis derives (60). Suppose that the derivation proceeds to the matrix v*P phase, in which the subject of Acc-*ing* is raised to Spec-V, where the unvalued case feature of the subject is valued as [ACC]. The lexical complex v*-*remember* excorporates and merges with the VP, projecting v*P, to whose specifier the matrix subject is merged.

(61)

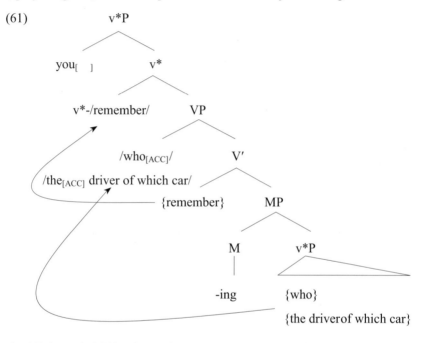

Both (60a) and (60b) share the same derivation and structure at this stage. From the next stage, however, their derivations diverge slightly. Let us first consider (60b): we should remember here that the matrix v* has an uninterpretable focus feature [uF], while the Spec-P of the raised subject has an interpretable counterpart. The PP *of which car* undergoes IM to the outer Spec-v* due to the uninterpretable [uF] of v*.

---

[16] I owe the grammaticality judgment of (60b) to Eloise Pearson (p.c.).

(62)

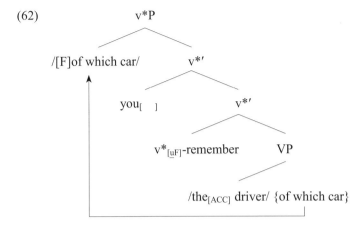

Notice here that IM of *of which car* from Spec-V does not violate the RIC, which states that the inactive elements are D and N. At the final CP phase, the PP *of which car* and the matrix subject *you* undergo IM to Spec-C and Spec-T, respectively.

(63) [$_{CP}$/of which car/[$_{C'}$ C-T-do[$_{TP}$/you$_{[NOM]}$/[$_{T'}$[$_{MP}$[$_{v*P}$ {of which car}[$_{v*'}$ {you}

 [$_{v*'}$ v*-/remember/ [$_{VP}$]]]]]]]]^{17}

Now let us turn to the derivation of (60a). In the matrix v*P phase, we have (64), where the accusative case is assigned to *who*, which is D, and an interpretable focus feature is assigned to Spec-D.

(64)

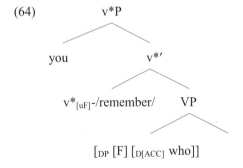

In (64), v* with [uF] locates *who* in its search space and attracts it to its

---

[17] We tentatively assume that the dummy *do* is generated in M(odal).

148 On Extraction from Subjects

outer Spec-v*. IM of *who* to Spec-v* apparently violates the RIC, because *who* is D and the head of the A-chain, which is case-assigned. The RIC prohibits D and N, which are case-assigned, from undergoing IM. In order to solve this difficulty, we should go back to the derivation, where the matrix VP is constructed and the subject of Acc-*ing* stays in the embedded Spec-v*.

(65)

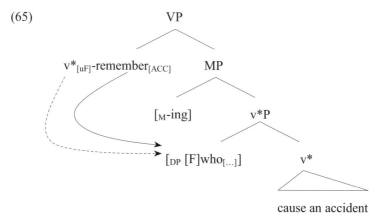

cause an accident

As shown in (65), v*$_{[uF]}$ and the main verb *remember* "see" the subject *who* at the same time. In the next stage of the derivation, the subject of the clausal gerund is raised to Spec-V for case-theoretic reasons.

(66)

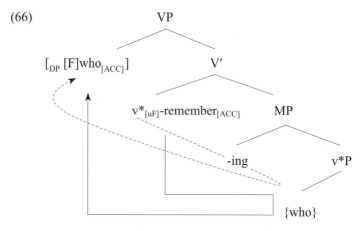

Recall here that we assume that the syntactic relation that holds in an earlier stage of the derivation will still hold at a later stage. In (66) the syntactic relation that holds in (65) also holds in (66): the phase head $v^*_{[uF]}$ and the main verb *remember* "see" the subject of the clausal gerund in Spec-V. In the next stage of the derivation, v^* excorporates and merges with VP to form a projection of v^*, with the matrix subject merged to Spec-v^*.

(67)

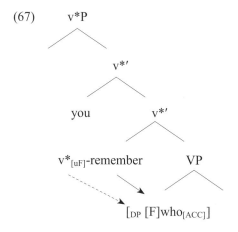

We assume that the syntactic relation that held in the earlier stage of the derivation also holds at the present stage: in (67), v^* and the main verb *remember* "see" *who* in Spec-V. In (67), seen from the v^* part of the lexical complex v^*-*remember*, the case-assigned subject *who* in Spec-V is considered to be in A-bar-position, not in A-position. In other words, the subject *who* in (67) heads a trivial A-bar chain, which means that IM of *who* can be successfully implemented without violating the RIC.

(68)

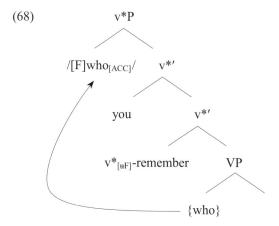

Here, in the matrix CP phase, after excorporation and subsequent merge of the lexical complex C-T-M (*do*), the matrix subject *you* and the interrogative subject of the clausal gerund are raised to Spec-T and Spec-C, respectively.

(69) [$_{CP}$/[F]Who/ [$_{C'}$ C$_{[uF]}$-T-M(do) [$_{TP}$ /you/ [$_{MP}$ [$_{v*P}$ {who} [$_{v*'}$ {you}

[$_{v*'}$ v*-remember

4.4.2. Extraction from a Subject of a Perceptual or Causative Construction

Matsubara (2008) makes some interesting observations concerning extraction from a subject (as he abbreviates it, ES) in perceptual and causative constructions. ES is possible from these two types of construction, as shown in (70) below.

(70) a. Of which planet$_i$ did you see [a picture t_i] hit the president (when it fell off the wall)?
 b. Of which car$_i$ did you make [the driver t_i] report himself to the police? (Matsubara (2008: 466–467))

Before examining how our Excorporation Analysis explains the grammaticality of (70), it is instructive to review Matsubara's analysis of the structure and derivation of these two constructions. He claims that the subject of a perceptual or causative infinitival subject undergoes raising to a matrix Spec-V for case-theoretic reasons, showing the relative word order of the infinitival subject and an adverb modifying the matrix verb.

(71) a. I saw John *probably* talking to Mary — certainly, John was (talking to Mary).
 b. We will make John *definitely* go to London — undoubtedly, John will (go to London). (Ibid.: 467)

In (71), the infinitival subjects that are base-generated in embedded Spec-v* undergo raising to the matrix Spec-V through Spec-T. Taking (71a) as an example, let us then see how Matsubara analyzes (71). In the matrix v*P phase, we have the following derivation and structure. (We assume that the adverb *probably* is adjoined to the matrix VP.)

(72) [$_{v*P}$ I [$_{v*}$ v*-saw [$_{VP}$ John [$_{V'}$ probably [$_{V'}$ saw [$_{TP}$ John [$_{T'}$ T [$_{v*P}$ John

The embedded subject *John* is raised successively from the embedded Spec-v* to the matrix Spec-V through Spec-T, and the unvalued case feature of the infinitival subject *John* is valued in the matrix Spec-V. We should note here that the infinitival subject *John* is still active in Spec-T, because the uninterpretable features, especially the case feature, are not checked yet.[18]

Having observed that infinitival subjects of perceptual and causative constructions undergo raising to a matrix VP for case-theoretic reasons, let us now consider the matter of ES from the infinitival subjects, taking (70a) as an example. In the matrix v*P phase, we have the following derivation and structure.

(73) [$_{v*P}$ I [$_{v*'}$ v*$_{[EF]}$-saw$_i$ [$_{VP}$ a picture of which planet [$_{V'}$ t$_i$ [$_{TP}$ a picture of which planet [$_{T'}$ T [$_{v*P}$ a picture of which planet [$_{v*}$ hit the president]]]]]]]]

In (73), there are three copies of *a picture of which planet*: one in the matrix Spec-V, another in Spec-T, and a third in the embedded Spec-v*. In the next stage of the derivation, the matrix v* with the Edge Feature (EF) attracts a *wh*-phrase *of which car* to its specifier position. The attraction from the embedded Spec-v* is prohibited by the Locality Condition: v* with [EF] cannot access the *wh*-phrase because the latter is embedded in the lower phase, which has already passed in the derivation. Attraction from the matrix Spec-V is to be excluded as a violation of the Inactivity Condition. Thus, the attraction of a *wh*-phrase takes place from Spec-T, where no uninterpretable features of the DP are checked.

---

[18] We should note here that Matsubara does not identify an intermediate Spec position as Spec-T. Perceptual and causative subjects behave differently from ECM subjects with regard to binding conditions and the license of Negative Polarity Items.
   (i) a. *I saw [the men$_i$ screw up the mission] because of each other's$_i$ blunders.
      b. I saw/heard [him$_i$ tell a lie/cry] before Bob's$_i$ mother did.
      c. I saw/heard [him$_i$ tell a lie/cry] even more clearly than Bob's$_i$ mother did.
      d. *I saw/heard [no applicants complain] after failing any of the tests.
                                                   (Matsubara (2008: 468))
The data in (i) seem to suggest that infinitival subjects do not raise to a higher position than adjunct clauses. However, we tentatively assume that infinitival subjects raise to a matrix Spec-V, leaving the problem raised by (i) for future research.

(74) [v*P of which planet [v* you [v*' v*[EF]-saw [VP a picture <of which planet>

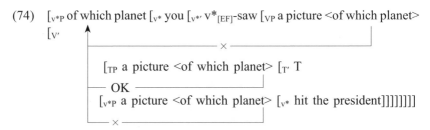

In the final stage of the derivation, the *wh*-phrase successfully undergoes IM to the matrix Spec-C.

(75) [CP Of which planet [C' C[EF]-did [TP you [v*P [v*' see [VP a picture [TP T [v*P hit the president]]]]]]]]

Now let us examine how our Excorporation Analysis analyzes (70a). Our analysis derives (70a) in a slightly different manner from the one presented from (73) to (75). As argued in the previous section, *wh*-extraction takes place from Spec-V directly. In an earlier stage of the derivation, we have (76), where the embedded infinitival clause consists of the MP, whose head is occupied with an abstract infinitival particle, and the subject of the embedded infinitival clause is raised to Spec-V for case-theoretic reasons.

(76)

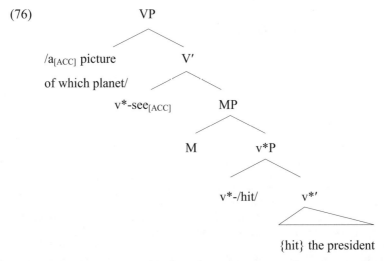

In the next stage of the derivation, the matrix v* undergoes excorporation and subsequent merge with VP, pied-piping phonetic materials for the main verb *see*, with an external argument *you* merged to Spec-v*.

(77)

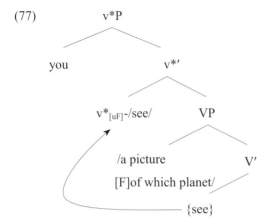

Recall that the phase head v* has an interpretable feature [uF] that triggers IM of a *wh*-element to its Spec, and that the interpretable counterpart is assigned to Spec-P. As a result, v* with the uninterpretable [uF] locates the PP *of which planet* in Spec-V and attracts it to Spec-v*.

(78) [$_{v*P}$ /[F] of which planet/ [$_{v*'}$ you [$_{v*'}$ v*-/see/ [$_{VP}$ /a picture {of which planet}

This IM of PP to Spec-v* apparently violates the Inactivity Condition, because PP-extraction takes place from Spec-V, in which DP is assigned accusative case. However, we must remember that we have adopted the RIC, which states that the D and N parts of a DP become inactive when unvalued case is valued and elements other than these two parts are inactive. Thus, the RIC allows the PP *of which planet* to be extracted from a case-assigned DP.

Before concluding this section, we should consider the total extraction of the embedded subject from these predicates.

(79) a. Which picture did you see hit the president?
     b. Which driver did you make report himself to the police?

Since these two constructions share the same derivation and structure, we will take (79a) as an example covering both and analyze it. Suppose that the derivation proceeds to (80), where the matrix VP is constructed in terms of excorporation and subsequent merge of v*-*see* to MP, whose head M is a part of the lexical complex v*-*see*-M.

(80) [$_{VP}$ v*$_{[uF]}$-see$_{[ACC]}$ [$_{MP}$ M [$_{v*P}$ [[F]which$_{[...]}$ picture] [$_{v*'}$ v*-/hit/ [$_{VP}$ ...]]]]]

In the next stage of the derivation, the embedded subject *which picture* is raised to Spec-V for case-theoretic reasons.

(81) [$_{VP}$ /[F]which$_{[ACC]}$ picture/ [$_{V'}$ v*$_{[uF]}$-see [$_{MP}$ M [$_{v*P}$ {which picture} [$_{v*'}$ v*-hit]]]]]

In the following stage, v*$_{[uF]}$-*see* excorporates and merges with VP, forming the projection of v*, and the matrix subject is merged to Spec-v*.

(82) [$_{v*P}$ you [$_{v*'}$ v*$_{[uF]}$-see [$_{VP}$ /which$_{[F][ACC]}$ picture/ [$_{V'}$ v*$_{[uF]}$-see [$_{MP}$ M [$_{v*P}$ {which picture} [$_{v*'}$ v*-hit]]]]]]

The matrix v*, with an uninterpretable [uF], then locates a *wh*-phrase in Spec-V and attracts it to Spec-v*.

(83) [$_{v*P}$ /[F]which picture/ [$_{v*'}$ you [$_{v*'}$ v*$_{[uF]}$-see [$_{VP}$ {which picture} [$_{V'}$ v*$_{[uF]}$-see [$_{MP}$ M [$_{v*P}$ {which picture} [$_{v*'}$ v*-hit]]]]]]

As mentioned above, although IM of a case-assigned *wh*-phrase apparently violates the RIC, this operation can nevertheless be implemented by the syntactic relation established in the earlier stage as (80), now slightly modified to (84).

(84) [$_{VP}$ v*$_{[uF]}$-see$_{[ACC]}$ [$_{MP}$ M [$_{v*P}$ [[F]which$_{[...]}$ picture] [$_{v*'}$ v*-hit [$_{VP}$ ...]]]]]

In (84), the main verb *see* with a case feature [ACC] and the light verb with a focus feature [uF] "see" the *wh*-phrase in the embedded Spec-v* at the same time, and identify it as being in A-position and A-bar-position, respectively. Furthermore, this syntactic relation is retained throughout the derivation. Thus, in (83) v* with [uF] identifies the case-assigned *wh*-phrase in Spec-V as the trivial head of an A-bar chain, and as a result the *wh*-phrase is extracted without violation of the RIC, which is sensitive to elements at the head of an A-chain, not an A-bar chain.

In the matrix CP phase, which is constructed by excorporation and subsequent merge of C-T-*did*, the *wh*-phrase is raised to the matrix Spec-C, where the uninterpretable focus feature [uF] of the matrix C is checked.

(85) [$_{CP}$ /[F]which picture/ [$_{C'}$ C$_{[uF]}$-did [$_{TP}$ /you/ [$_{v*P}$ {which picture} [$_{v*'}$ {you}

Chapter 5

Extraction from Subjects of Passive and Unaccusative Predicates

This chapter will take up total extraction and subextraction from subjects of passive predicates and unaccusative predicates, discussing some consequences of the Excorporation Analysis and the Revised Inactivity Condition for extraction from subjects.

5.1. Extraction from Subjects of Passive Predicates

In Chapter 2, we have seen that subextraction of a *wh*-phrase from the subjects of active matrix sentences is impossible, as demonstrated in (1a) below, and we have discussed the fact that (1b), where no extraction occurs, is a grammatical counterpart to (1a) and examined how it can be derived.

(1) a. *Of which car will the driver cause a scandal?
    b. The driver of which car will cause a scandal?

Unlike in the *wh*-phrase from the subject of the active matrix sentence in (1), subextraction is possible from the subjects of passive matrix predicates, as shown in (2a) below.

(2) a. Of which car was the driver arrested?   (Radford (2009: 410))
    b. The driver of which car was arrested?

In this section, we will examine how our Excorporation Analysis can account for the grammatical difference between (1) and (2).

Before going into the analysis of (2), we need to examine how our Excorporation Analysis derives passive sentences; this derivation is demonstrated in Egashira and Tonoike (2012), which takes (3) as an example.

(3)　The city was destroyed (by the enemy).

(Egashira and Tonoike (2012))

We postulated in Egashira and Tonoike (2012) a light adjective α that constitutes a lexical complex with a verb, and plays two roles in such a complex: it absorbs the case feature of the verb (cf. Jaeggli (1986)), and determines its morphological form.[1]

(4)　destroy [ACC] → α-destroy-*ed* [ACC]

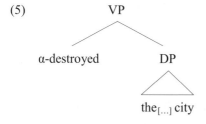

In an earlier stage of the derivation of (3), we have (4), where the light adjective α and the verb *destroy* constitute a lexical complex, taking *the city* as the complement of the verb, as in (5).

(5)
```
              VP
             /  \
      α-destroyed  DP
                   /\
                the[...] city
```

In the next stage of the derivation, α excorporates and merges with VP to form a projection of α with which a lexical complex C-T-*be* is merged, thus forming a projection of *be*:[2]

---

[1] Absorption of case is marked by a strikethrough in (4).
[2] We assume that *be* is given the form *was* by the tense feature [+Past] of T.

Chapter 5 Extraction from Subjects of Passive and Unaccusative Predicates 157

(6)
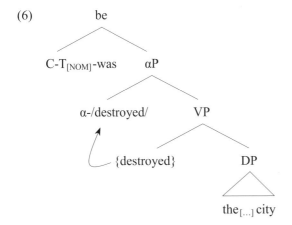

In the next stage of the derivation, T with case feature [NOM] excorporates and merges with the projection of *be*, pied-piping with the phonetic form *was* in accordance with the Overt Syntax Hypothesis; and the DP *the city*, which is the complement of the verb *destroy*, is attracted to Spec-T for case-theoretic reasons.

(7)
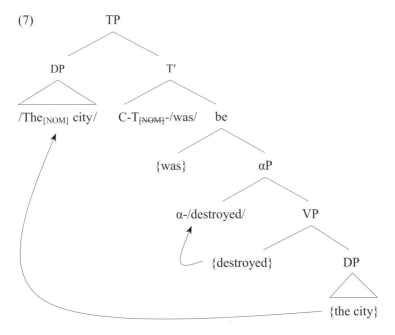

In (7), the complement of the verb *the city* is case-assigned in Spec-T. This is the way the derivation of passives proceeds under the Excorporation Analyis.

Armed with the assumption above, let us turn to (2), where a *wh*-phrase is successfully subextracted from the subject. It is helpful to recall the discussion in Chapter 2, where we have argued, following Tonoike (2000), that *wh*-movment is driven by the need to check the focus feature [F], and have assumed that an uninterpretable focus feature [uF] is assigned to a phase head while an interpretable focus feature [F] is assigned to specifier position of a moved phrase, including a *wh*-phrase itself. Thus, in (2a), an interpretable focus feature [F] is assigned to Spec-P and in (2b) to Spec-D.

(8) a. [$_{DP}$ the driver [$_{PP}$ [F]of which car]]
 b. [$_{DP}$ [F] the driver of which car]

In an earlier stage of the derivation of (2a), we have (9), where the lexical complex α-*arrest* is merged with *the driver of which car*, forming the projection of V, as demonstrated in (9a), and α with the phonetic form /arrested/ excorporates and merges with the VP, to form a projection of α, as represented in (9b).

(9) a. [$_{VP}$ α-arrested [$_{DP}$ the driver [$_{PP}$ [F]of which car]]]
 b. [$_{αP}$ α-/arrested/ [$_{VP}$ {arrested} [$_{DP}$ the driver [$_{PP}$ [F]of which car]]]]

In the next stage of the derivation, the lexical complex C-T-*was* is merged with the structure in (9b), to form a projection of *be*, as demonstrated in (10a); and further excorporation and merge of the lexical complex C-T-*was* take place, forming a projection of T, to whose specifier position the complement of the verb *the driver of which car* is attracted for case-theoretic reasons, as represented in (10b).

(10) a. [$_{be}$ C-T$_{[NOM]}$-was [$_{αP}$ α-/arrested/ [$_{VP}$ [$_{DP}$ the$_{[...]}$ driver [$_{PP}$ [F]of which car]]]]]^3
 b. [$_{TP}$ [$_{DP}$ the$_{[NOM]}$ driver [$_{PP}$ [F]of which car]] [$_{T'}$ C-T$_{[NOM]}$-/was/ [$_{be}$ {was} [$_{αP}$ α-/arrested/ [$_{VP}$ {$_{DP}$ the driver [$_{PP}$ [F]of which car]}]]]]]

In (10b), the unvalued case feature of *the driver of which car* is valued as [NOM]. In the next stage of the derivation, C, pied-piping T and /was/, excorporates and merges with the TP to form the projection of C. It should be remembered here that the C, which is a phase head, has an uninterpretable

---

^{3} I leave out the meaning of the verb {arrest} in (10a).

Chapter 5 Extraction from Subjects of Passive and Unaccusative Predicates   159

[uF].

(11)

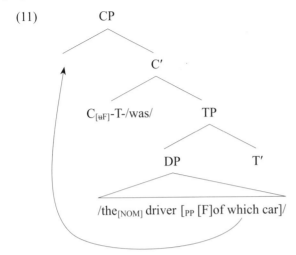

In (11), C with [uF] serves as a probe and locates a PP in the DP situated in Spec-T, as a result of which the PP *of which car* is attracted to Spec-C and the uninterpretable focus feature of C is checked and deleted. We should recall here that the attraction does not violate the Revised Inactivity Condition (RIC), which states that case-assigned D and N are invisible to further computation. In (11), the D is case-assigned but the PP is not. Hence, we can successfully derive (2a).

Let us turn now to the case of (2b), which can be derived if (8b), where an interpretable focus feature [F] is assigned to Spec-D, is chosen as a complement of the verb *arrest*. Let us suppose that the derivation then proceeds to (12), where an αP is constructed by excorporation and subsequent merge of the lexical complex α-*arrested*.

(12) [αP α-/arrested/ [VP {arrested} [DP [F]the driver of which car]]]

The lexical complex C-T-*was* is merged with the αP in (12) to form the projection headed by *be* (=*was*), as seen in (13a). Next, T excorporates, pied-piping C and a phonetic form /*was*/, and merges with the projection of *be*, forming a projection of T, as observed in (13b), with the DP *the driver of which car* attracted to Spec-T for case-theoretic reasons, as shown in (13c).

(13) a. [$_{be}$ C-T$_{[NOM]}$-was [$_{\alpha P}$ α-/arrested/ [$_{VP}$ [$_{DP}$ [F] the$_{[...]}$ driver of which car]]]]
b. [$_{TP}$ C-T$_{[NOM]}$-/was/ [$_{be}$ {was} [$_{\alpha P}$ α-/arrested/ [$_{VP}$ [$_{DP}$ [F] the$_{[...]}$ driver of which car]]]]]
c. [$_{TP}$ /[F] the$_{[NOM]}$ driver of which car/ [$_{T'}$ C-T$_{[NOM]}$-/was/ [$_{be}$ [$_{\alpha P}$ α-/arrested/ [$_{VP}$ {the driver of which car}]]]]]

We need to remember here that the matrix complemetizer C has an uninterpretable feature [uF] to be checked, and that it can enter into a checking relation with an interpretable [F] carried by the subject without further excorporation and merge of the lexical complex C-T-/was/. This also means that the topmost projection in (12b) is not only TP but also CP.

(14) a. [$_{CP/TP}$ [F] /the driver$_{[NOM]}$ of which car/ [$_{C'/T'}$ C$_{[uF]}$-T$_{[NOM]}$-/was/ [$_{be}$ {was} [$_{\alpha P}$ α-/arrested/ [$_{VP}$ {the driver of which car}]]]]]
b.

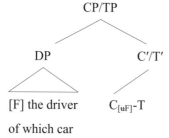

It would be possible for C-T-/was/ to undergo further excorporation and merge, to form a projection of C, to whose specifier the subject is attracted.

(15) [$_{CP}$ [F] /the driver$_{[NOM]}$ of which car/ [$_{C'}$ C$_{[uF]}$-T-/was/ [$_{TP}$ t$_i$ [$_{T'}$ t$_j$[4]

As argued in Chapter 2, (15) is excluded in favor of (14) for reasons of derivational economy: (14) contains fewer operations than (15).

At this point, we should compare *wh*-extraction from subjects of active sentences with that from subjects of passive sentences. As observed in the comparison of (1) and (2), repeated below as (16), subextraction of a *wh*-phrase from the subjects of active sentences is banned.

---

[4] In (15), copies that should be represented as {...} are replaced by a trace *t* for ease of exposition.

Chapter 5 Extraction from Subjects of Passive and Unaccusative Predicates 161

(16) a. *Of which car will the driver cause a scandal?
   b. The driver of which car will cause a scandal?
   c. Of which car was the driver arrested?
   d. The driver of which car was arrested?

The grammatical differences observed in (16) can be explained by the structural difference between passive and active sentences, and by the checking relation that holds among focus features. Let us briefly look at this issue. As argued in Chapter 2, the matrix v* has a θ-feature to be discharged on the subject DP and an uninterpretable feature [uF] to be checked. The only derivation that satisfies both these features at the same time, especially [uF], is to merge the DP whose topmost Spec-D is assigned [F].

(17)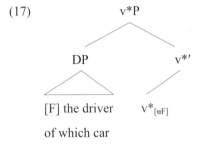

In (17), the uninterpretable [uF] of v* is checked by the interpretable counterpart that the subject carries in the Spec–head relation. In the final stage of the derivation, the subject DP is raised to Spec-T for case-theoretic reasons, where the uninterpretable [uF] of the matrix C undergoes checking at the same time.

(18) [$_{CP/TP}$ [F] /the$_{[NOM]}$ driver of which car/ [$_{C'/T'}$ C$_{[uF]}$-T$_{[NOM]}$-/will/ [$_{MP}$ {will}

Thus, the derivation successfully converges in (18).

If an interpretable feature [F] were assigned to another specifier position than the topmost Spec-D, the derivations would crash at the v*P phase. Suppose that an interpretable focus feature [F] is assigned to a Spec-P contained in the subject DP, and that the DP is merged with Spec-v* for θ-theoretic reasons.

(19)

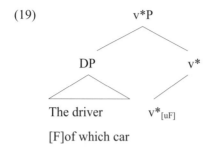

In (19), when the subject DP is merged with v*, the interpretable focus feature [F] of the subject DP cannot check the uninterpretable focus feature [uF] of v* because they are not in a checking configuration: the interpretable [F] is deeply embedded in the subject phrase. Thus, the derivation crashes in this phase, and (16a) will never be generated in our framework.

However, as observed above, in the passive sentence there is no phase head v*, and the passive subject is generated in a position lower than a phase head (matrix C) with an uninterpretable focus feature [uF]. This assumption makes it possible to generate an interpretable [F] feature in the topmost Spec-D.

As a final remark on this matter, we will examine an alternative derivation for (2), which is repeated below as (20).

(20) a. Of which car was the driver arrested?
b. The driver of which car was arrested?

As described above, Egashira and Tonoike (2012) introduce the functional head α for passive sentences. The roles that this functional head α plays are the morphological realization and case absorption of the verb that α constitutes a lexical complex with. In addition, let us assume that α is assigned [uF], but that, contrary to Legate (2003), α is not a phase head. It then follows that we have (21) in an earlier stage of the derivation of (20).

(21) a. [$_{αP}$ α$_{[uF]}$-/arrested/ [$_{VP}$ {arrested} [$_{DP}$ the$_{[...]}$ driver [$_{PP}$ [F]of which car]]]]
b. [$_{αP}$ α$_{[uF]}$-/arrested/ [$_{VP}$ {arrested} [$_{DP}$ [F] the$_{[...]}$ driver of which car]]]

In (21), an uninterpretable focus feature [uF] is assigned to the functional head α, and an interpretable counterpart is assigned to the Spec-P contained in the subject phrase in (21a) and to the topmost Spec-D in (21b). The uninterpretable focus feature [uF] serves as a probe and locates the interpre-

Chapter 5 Extraction from Subjects of Passive and Unaccusative Predicates   163

table counterpart [F]. The α in (21a) attracts the PP *of which car* into its Spec, and that in (21b), the DP *the driver of which car*.

(22) a. [$_{αP}$ /[F]of which car/ [$_{α'}$α$_{[uF]}$-/arrested/ [$_{VP}$ [$_{DP}$ the$_{[...]}$ driver {of which car}]]]]

b. [$_{αP}$ /[F] the$_{[...]}$ driver of which car/ [$_{α'}$α$_{[uF]}$-/arrested/ [$_{VP}$ [$_{DP}$ {the driver of which car}]]]]

In (22), the uninterpretable focus feature [uF] is checked and deleted successfully. In the next stage of the derivation, a lexical complex C-T-*was* is merged with the αP to form a projection of *be*, followed by excorporation and merge of C-T-/*was*/ to form a projection of T.

(23) a. [$_{TP}$ C$_{[uF]}$-T$_{[NOM]}$-/was/ [$_{be}$ {was} [$_{αP}$ /[F]of which car/ [$_{α'}$ α$_{[uF]}$-/arrested/ [$_{VP}$ [$_{DP}$ the driver$_{[...]}$ {of which car}]]]]]]

b. [$_{TP}$ C$_{[uF]}$-T$_{[NOM]}$-/was/ [$_{be}$ {was} [$_{αP}$ /[F] the driver$_{[...]}$ of which car/ [$_{α'}$ α$_{[uF]}$-/arrested/ [$_{VP}$ [$_{DP}$ {the driver of which car}]]]]]]

The two derivations diverge at this point; let us first consider the derivation of (23b). Here, the passive subject *the driver of which car* in Spec-α is attracted to Spec-T for case-theoretic reasons, as demonstrated in (24).

(24) a. [$_{TP}$ /[F] the$_{[NOM]}$ driver of which car/ [$_{T'}$ C$_{[uF]}$-T$_{[NOM]}$-/was/ [$_{be}$ {was} [$_{αP}$ {the driver of which car}[$_{α'}$ α$_{[uF]}$-/arrested/ [$_{VP}$ [$_{DP}$ {the driver of which car}]]]]]]]

b.

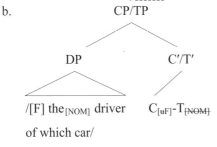

The unvalued case feature [...] of the passive subject is valued in the configuration of (24b) above. It is also possible to check the uninterpretable focus feature of C in this configuration. However, further excorporation and merge of C-T are not operative, for the same reason mentioned above.

Let us turn to (23b), repeated here as (25).

(25) [TP C[uF]-T[NOM]-/was/ [be {was} [αP /[F]of which car/ [α' α[uF]-/arrested/ [VP [DP the[...] driver {of which car}]]]]]]

In (25), C and T, each with an uninterpretable feature to be checked, function as probes and locate their goals: T[NOM] locates the DP in the complement position of the verb *arrested*, and C[uF] locates the PP in Spec-α. Primarily, T[NOM] attracts the passive subject to its Spec, as demonstrated below.

(26) [TP /The[NOM] driver {of which car}/ [T' C[uF]-T[NOM]-/was/ [be [αP /[F]of which car/ [α' α[uF]-/arrested/ [VP {the driver[...]} {of which car}}]]]]]]

In (26), the unvalued case feature [...] of the passive subject is valued as [NOM]. Although at the stage of (25), the C with [uF] located a *wh*-phrase in Spec-α, it did not attract the goal in Spec-α because Spec-T, be it outer or inner, is not a scope position for a *wh*-phrase. It then follows that the C with [uF] excorporates and merges with the TP to form a projection of C, to whose specifier the *wh*-phrase in Spec-α is merged.

(27)

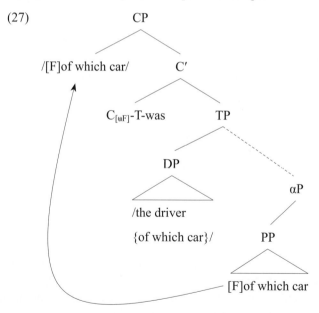

C[uF] cannot access the PP *of which car* inside the DP situated in Spec-T because the latter does not have a phonetic form, only a semantic form (as indicated by the curly brackets), and the Overt Syntax Hypothesis prevents

Chapter 5   Extraction from Subjects of Passive and Unaccusative Predicates   165

Internal Merge (movement) of elements without a phonetic form.

We have observed here that our Excorporation Analysis yields correct passive sentences that include extraction from a subject. I would like to leave open for future research the question of which of the two derivations is more appropriate.

5.2. Extraction from Subjects of Unaccusative Predicates

This section will examine how our Excorporation Analysis, coupled with the RIC, analyzes *wh*-extraction from the subject of an unaccusative predicate and also from an associate DP of a *there*-construction, as demonstrated below.

(28) a. Of which drugs did traces remain in the blood?
b. Of which drugs did there remain traces in the blood?

(Radford (2009: 437))

According to Radford (2009), it is possible for a *wh*-phrase to be subextracted from the subject of an unaccusative predicate; (28a) and (28b) are similar in that the *wh*-phrase *of which drugs* is subextracted from the subject or the associate of the unaccusative verb *remain*, but they differ in that (28b) contains the expletive *there* whereas (28a) does not. Regarding the derivation of structures that contain an unaccusative verb, we assume that an accusative verb constitutes a lexical complex with a functional unaccusative light v, forming v-V, and that this complex constitutes a further lexical complex with Pred: v-V-Pred. (The functional head Pred was first proposed by Bowers (1993).) Although we basically follow Bowers in that we consider this functional head to mediate the predication relation, we differ slightly in that we consider Pred to be a head of a small clause that denotes the existence in a certain place of the subject of the unaccusative verb. For instance, declarative counterparts to (28) denote existence of *traces of drugs* in the blood.

(29) a. Traces of drugs remain in the blood.
b. There remain traces of drugs in the blood.

Above, (29a) and (29b) share the same derivation until PredP is constructed; let us see how this is done. The functional head Pred merges with a locative PP to form a projection of Pred, to whose specifier the subject DP is merged.

(30)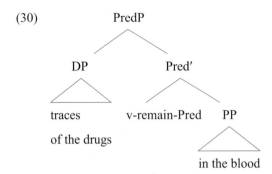

We assume that the subject DP has a null D that has an unvalued case feature [...].

(31) [$_{DP}$ D$_{[...]}$ traces of the drugs]

The derivations of (29a) and (29b) diverge at this point. Let us observe (29a) first. After PredP is constructed, the main verb *remain* excorporates and merges with PredP to form a projection of the V, followed by excorporation and merge of the unaccusative light verb v with a phonetic shape /remain/.

(32)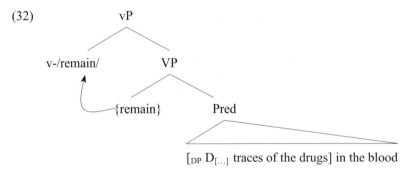

In the next stage of the derivation, the C-T complex is merged with the vP to form a projection of T. In this case, T has the case feature [NOM], which attracts the DP to Spec-T.

(33)

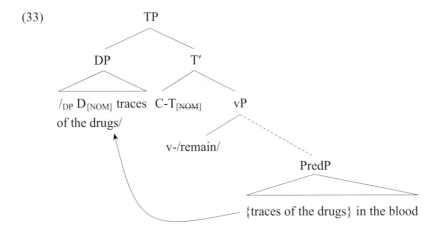

In (33), the unvalued case of the subject […] is valued as [NOM] in Spec-T.

With this derivation in mind, let us see how (28a) is derived. Here, an interpretable Focus feature [F] is assigned to Spec-P, which is contained in the Subject DP.

(34) [DP D[...] traces [PP[F] of which drugs]]

Now let us suppose that the derivation proceeds to the stage of the matrix TP, which is constructed by excorporation and merge of the lexical complex C-T-M(*did*) and Internal Merge of the subject to Spec-T, where an unvalued case feature of D is valued as [NOM].

(35)

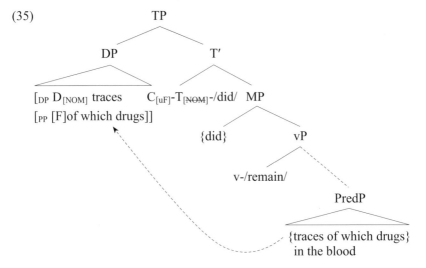

In (28a), C inherently has an uninterpretable focus feature [uF]. C with [uF] can serve as a probe and locate the *wh*-phrase in Spec-Pred; however, it cannot attract the *wh*-phrase for feature checking, because the elements in Spec-Pred do not have a phonetic shape. It then follows that the only element that can still check [uF] is the PP assigned [F] contained in the subject phrase in Spec-T. However, the *wh*-phrases in Spec-T and C are not in the checking relation. Thus, C excorporates and merges with the TP, forming a projection of C to whose Spec the *wh*-phrase is raised.

(36)

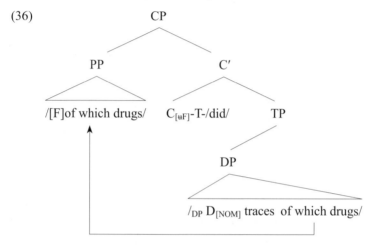

In (36), the *wh*-phrase in Spec-C and the head C are in a checking relation, and thus the uninterpretable focus feature of C is checked and deleted.

It is interesting here to note that if an interpretable focus feature [F] is assigned to the topmost Spec-D in the subject phrase, (37a) is derived.

(37) a. Traces of which drugs remained in the blood?
 b. [$_{CP/TP}$ [$_{DP}$ [F] D$_{[NOM]}$ Traces of which drugs [$_{C'/T'}$ C$_{[uF]}$-T$_{[NOM]}$-did ... [$_{PredP}$ {traces ...}

In this case, when the unaccusative subject is raised to Spec-T for case-theoretic reasons, an uninterpretable focus feature [uF] of C and the [F] of the subject enter into a checking relation. As a result, a grammatical sentence (37a) is obtained.

Now let us turn to (28b) and its declarative counterpart, which are repeated as (38a) and (38b), respectively.

Chapter 5 Extraction from Subjects of Passive and Unaccusative Predicates

(38) a. Of which drugs did there remain traces in the blood?
b. There remained traces of the drugs in the blood.

We assume, following Burzio (1986), Belletti (1988), and Levin and Rappaport Hovav (1995), among others, that the unaccusative verb *remain* here has a partitive case feature [PART] to be checked. Suppose that the derivation proceeds to a PredP. Let us begin with (38b).

(39)
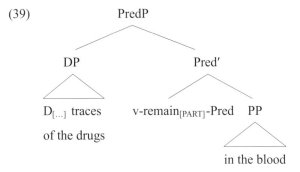

In the next stage of the derivation, the lexical complex v-*remain*$_{[PART]}$ excorporates and merges with the PredP to form a projection of the V.

(40)
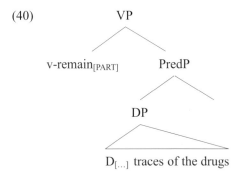

Recall that adopting the case-assigning mechanism proposed by Tonoike (1999), we have assumed that in English case is assigned under Merge to a case-assigning category. In the case of (40), the unaccusative verb *remain* has a case feature [PART] to assign to a DP, and thus the DP in Spec-Pred is attracted to Spec-V, with unvalued case feature [...] valued as [PART].

(41)

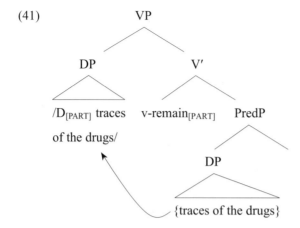

In the next stage, the lexical complex v-*remain* undergoes excorporation and merge with VP, forming a projection of the unaccusative light verb v; and following Deal (2009), expletive *there* is merged to Spec-vP.[5]

(42)

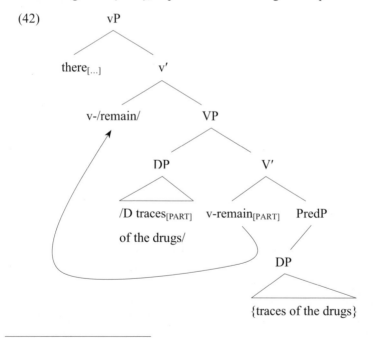

---

[5] Based on literature by Jackendoff (1996), Hay, Kennedy and Levin (1999), and Levin and Rappaport Hovav (2002), Deal proposes that a v that does not denote *cause* selects expletive *there*, and that this *there* is merged to Spec-v.

We also assume with Deal that expletive *there* has an unvalued case feature […], to be valued in the course of the derivation.[6]

Next, a matrix lexical complex C-T is merged to the vP, forming a projection of T. In this case, T has a case feature [NOM] that attracts expletive *there* in Spec-v, in accordance with English case-assignment system.[7]

(43)

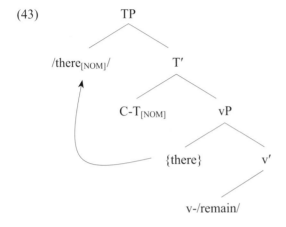

In (43), the unvalued case feature […] of the expletive *there* is valued as [NOM] by means of the agreement holding between T and the expletive.

Armed with this set of assumptions concerning the derivation of the construction with *there*, let us go back to (28b), repeated here as (44).

(44) Of which drugs did there remain traces in the blood?

Suppose that the derivation proceeds to (45), where the PredP, VP, and vP are constructed in the manner discussed above.

---

[6] As for the case where *there* is assigned, see Chomsky (1986b), Hoekstra and Mulder (1990), Lasnik (1992, 1995), and Groat (1995) for details.

[7] Although expletive *there* does not have semantic content, we tentatively assume that it leaves a copy behind in Spec-V, leaving open the issue of whether or not expletive *there* leaves behind a copy.

(45)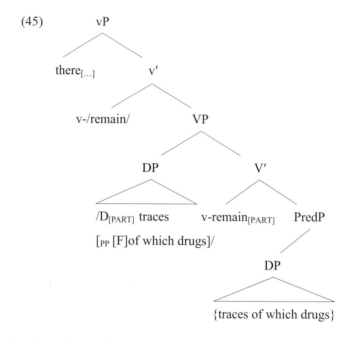

At this point it should be emphasized that the associate DP generated in Spec-Pred undergoes Internal Merge to Spec-VP, where its unvalued case feature gets valued as [PART]. It should also be pointed out that an interpretable focus feature [F] is assigned to the Spec-P contained in the Subject DP.

Suppose next that a lexical complex C-T-M (*did*) is merged with vP to form a projection of Modal, followed by excorporation and merge of C-T-*did* with the MP to whose specifier the expletive is raised for case-theoretic reasons.

(46)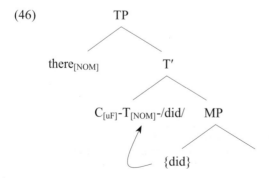

Chapter 5 Extraction from Subjects of Passive and Unaccusative Predicates   173

Recall here that the C is assigned an uninterpretable focus feature [uF], which forces the lexical complex C-T-*did* to excorporate and merge to the TP. The C with [uF] serves as a probe and locates the *wh*-phrase in Spec-V.

(47)

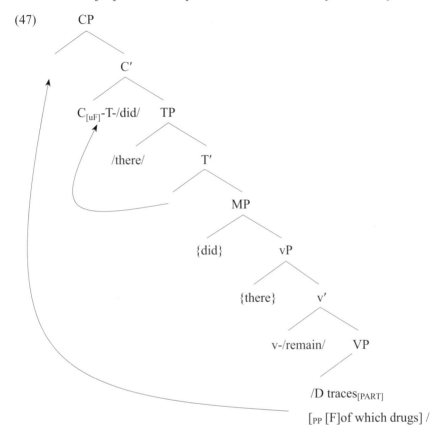

As argued throughout this book, attraction of a *wh*-phrase to Spec-C can be successfully implemented because the RIC is insensitive to movement of a PP, since the latter is not assigned case.

We have seen that our Excorporation Analysis can account for *wh*-sub-extraction from a subject of unaccusative verbs and that from an associate of a *there*-construction containing an unaccusative verb.

At this point, one prediction holds: that total extraction of the *wh*-phrase is impossible because the *wh*-phrase itself is D and case is assigned to D.

(48)   What did there remain in the blood?

In (48), the *wh*-phrase generated in Spec-Pred undergoes movement to Spec-V, where it is case-assigned by the unaccusative verb *remain*.

(49) [$_{VP}$ what$_{[PART]}$ [$_{V'}$ v-remain$_{[PART]}$ [$_{PredP}$ {what} Pred [$_{PP}$ in the blood]]]]

In (49), the *wh*-phrase, which is D, is assigned partitive case. This means that it becomes inactive and cannot undergo any further movement. However, grammaticality judgments on this vary from informant to informant, from grammatical to ungrammatical but not so bad.

One possible solution to this range of grammaticality judgments is to assume that (48) can be derived by multiple types of lexical complex. In one, six heads present at the same time constitute a lexical complex: $C_{[uF]}$-T-M (did)-v-V(remain$_{[PART]}$)-Pred. In this case, when the VP is constructed, $C_{[uF]}$ and remain$_{[PART]}$ "see" the *wh*-phrase *what* at the same time.

(50)

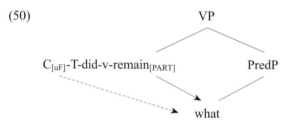

Remember that as argued in the previous chapter, the syntactic relation that has held in an earlier stage of the derivation will also hold in a later stage. It then follows that even when a *wh*-phrase is attracted to Spec-V, where partitive case is assigned, the C with [uF] can identify the *wh*-phrase as the trivial head of an A-bar-chain when the matrix CP is constructed.

(51) [$_{CP}$ $C_{[uF]}$-T-did [$_{TP}$ there [$_{MP}$ [$_{vP}$ v-remain [$_{VP}$ /what/ [$_{PredP}$ ...]]]]]]

This identification of the *wh*-phrase *what* as the (trivial) head of the A-bar chain enables *what* to be attracted to Spec-C without incurring violation of the RIC.

The other type of lexical complex that is involved in (48) and may lead it to be judged as ungrammatical is actually two separate lexical complexes: $C_{[uF]}$-T-*did* and v-*remain*-Pred, as discussed from (45) to (47). In this case, over the course of the derivation, $C_{[uF]}$ and remain$_{[PART]}$ never "see" the *wh*-phrase simultaneously in the course of the derivation. Thus, the *wh*-phrase cannot be extracted from Spec-V without violating the RIC.

A similar analysis to that proposed for (28) can also derive the following passive sentence in which *there* occurs.

(52) a. Of which drugs were there found traces?
 b. Of which drugs were traces found?

In 5.1 we have already examined how (52b) is derived, but it is helpful here to review the derivation of (52b). We assume that passive verbs form a lexical complex with the functional head α, i.e., α-V, and that this lexical complex merges with the complement of the verb to form a projection of V, followed by excorporation and merge of α with the VP, forming an αP.

(53) [$_{αP}$ α-/found/ [$_{VP}$ {found} traces of which drugs]]

In the next stage of the derivation, a lexical complex C-T-be is merged with the αP to form a projection of *be*, followed by excorporation and merge of T with the projection of *be* to form TP, to whose specifier the complement of the verb *traces of which drug* is merged internally.

(54) [$_{TP}$ /$_{DP}$ D$_{[NOM]}$ traces of which drugs/ [$_{T'}$ C-T$_{[NOM]}$-/were/ [$_{be}$ [$_{αP}$ α-/found/ [$_{VP}$ {traces of which drugs}]]]]]

In Spec-T, the derived subject is case-assigned. Notice here that an uninterpretable focus feature [uF] and an interpretable one are respectively assigned to C and Spec-P.

(55) [$_{TP}$ /$_{DP}$ D$_{[NOM]}$ traces [[F]of which drugs]/ [$_{T'}$ C$_{[uF]}$-T$_{[NOM]}$-were

In this configuration, the uninterpretable focus feature [uF] cannot be checked by the corresponding interpretable focus feature [F], and so the C excorporates and merges with the TP to form a projection of C.

(56)

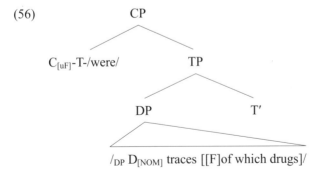

/$_{DP}$ D$_{[NOM]}$ traces [[F]of which drugs]/

The C with the uninterpretable focus feature [uF] serves as a probe and locates the PP *of which drugs*, and as a result, the PP undergoes Internal

Merge to Spec-CP, checking and deleting the [uF] of C.

(57)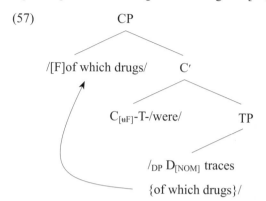

The extraction of the *wh*-phrase is not precluded by the RIC because the RIC only restricts movement of case-assigned D and N, and the extracted PP *of which car* is not case-assigned.

Now let us turn to (52a). This sentence is different from (52b) in that expletive *there* appears in the construction. This is strongly reminiscent of the unaccusative *there*-construction discussed above, in relation to which we argued that there are two kinds of unaccusative verbs: one with no case features and the other with a partitive case feature [PART],[8] and that functional head v, which is a part of the lexical complex v-unaccusative verb, selects expletive *there* (in the sense of Deal (2009)). Now let us suppose that α in passives, which is a part of the lexical complex α-V, has two roles to play: to absorb the accusative case feature of V, and to optionally assign partitive case [PART] to V after absorption of the accusative case. Let us suppose further that α hosts expletive *there* in its specifier position. Armed with these assumptions, let us examine how (52a) is derived.

First, in the lexical complex α-*found*, α assigns a partitive case feature to V, absorbing the accusative case feature of V.

(58) α-found$_{[ACC]}$ → α-found$_{[PART]}$

The lexical complex α-*found*$_{[PART]}$ merges with the complement of the verb to form a projection of V.

---

[8] We assume that while the unaccusative verb *remain* in (29) has no case feature, that in (38) has a partitive case feature [PART].

Chapter 5   Extraction from Subjects of Passive and Unaccusative Predicates   177

(59)

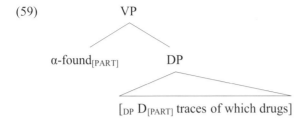

[DP D[PART] traces of which drugs]

In accordance with our case-assignment system, which is repeated below as (60), the unvalued case feature [...] of D is valued as [PART] when α-*found*[PART] and the complement of the verb merge.

(60) In English, case is assigned under Merge to the case-assigning category.

In the next stage of the derivation, α excorporates and merges with the VP, pied-piping the phonetic shape of *found*, to form the projection of α, to whose specifier expletive *there* is merged.

(61)

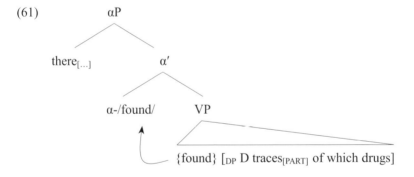

Notice here that the expletive *there* has an unvalued case feature [...]. In the next stage of the derivation, the lexical complex C-T-*be* is merged to αP, to form a projection of *be*, followed by excorporation of C-T-/were/, forming a TP. We should remember that T has a nominative case feature, which drives movement of expletive *there* to Spec-T from Spec-α.

(62)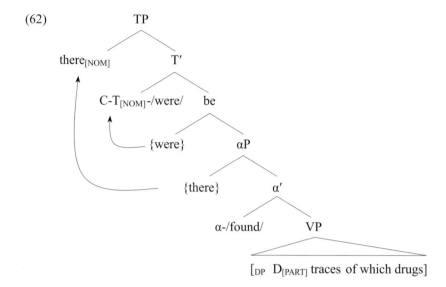

In (62), the expletive *there* is case-assigned by being merged with the case-assigning category T. In this case, C has an uninterpretable focus feature [uF], and the Spec-P included in the associate DP has an interpretable counterpart. The uninterpretable focus feature C with [uF] serves as a probe and locates the PP in the associate, as a result of which the PP is attracted to Spec-C.

(63)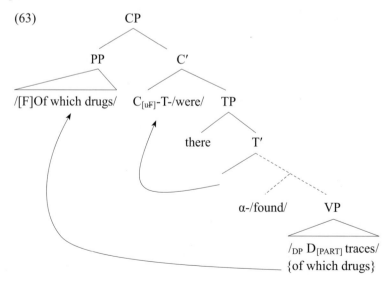

In (63), the uninterpretable focus feature [uF] is checked and deleted by its interpretable counterpart in Spec-C. Thus, we can successfully derive (52a). It goes without saying that movement of the PP *of which drugs* does not violate the RIC, which prohibits movement of case-assigned D or N.

5.3. Extraction from the Unaccusative Predicate *arrive*

In this section, we will analyze the following two sentences in which total extraction and subextraction occur from the associate of the unaccusative verb *arrive*.

(64) a. *Who did there arrive? (Chomsky (2014))
 b. Of which car did there arrive a driver?[9]

Contrary to the construction discussed in 5.2, a clear grammaticality difference can be found between (64a) and (64b). There seem to be two possible ways to exclude (64a). One is to resort to the definiteness effect, which restricts occurrence of definite noun phrases in *there*-construction. As pointed out by Milsark (1974), Safir (1985), and Lumsden (1988), among others, a noun phrase that appears in a *there*-construction must be an indefinite noun.

(65) a. There is a man in the room. (Safir (1985: 92))
 b. *There is the man in the room. (Ibid.)

If interrogative *who* has a function that picks up from a set of persons someone that a speaker wants to identify, *who* can be interpreted as a definite noun.[10] It then follows that (64a) can be excluded in the same way as (65b).

The other way to rule out (64a) (but rule in (64b)) is to resort to the RIC. Let us observe how these two sentences are analyzed in terms of the Excorporation Analysis. We can apply the same analysis proposed in 5.1 to (64). As assumed in the previous section, unaccusative V constitutes a lexical complex with v and Pred: v-*arrive*-Pred. Now let us suppose that there is an implicit locative expression PP, in (64), and that it is generated as a complement of Pred.

With this in mind, let us tackle (64a). In the early stage of the derivation of (64a), we have (66), where PredP is constructed by merge of an im-

---

[9] I owe to Eloise Pearson the judgment of this sentence as grammatical.
[10] I am thankful to Shigeo Tonoike (p.c.) for drawing my attention to this fact.

plicit complement PP, which is represented in outline font, and merge of an associate DP as specifier.

(66)

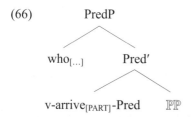

In the next stage of the derivation, the lexical complex v-*arrive* excorporates and merges with PredP to form a projection of V, to whose specifier the interrogative *who*, which is introduced with an unvalued case feature [...], moves to get partitive case.

(67)

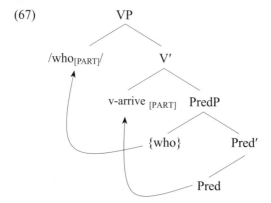

In (67), the unvalued case feature of *who* is valued and thus it becomes inactive. Suppose that the unaccusative light verb v excorporates and merges with the VP to form a projection of v, to whose specifier *there* is merged.

(68)

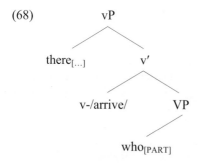

Chapter 5   Extraction from Subjects of Passive and Unaccusative Predicates   181

In the following stage of the derivation, a lexical complex C-T-M(*did*) is merged to form an MP, followed by excorporation and merge of T, forming a projection of T to whose specifier *there* is attracted.

(69)

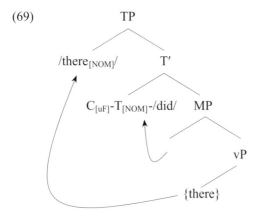

In (69), the unvalued case feature of *there* is valued as [NOM]. C in this case has an uninterpretable focus feature [uF] to be checked.

In the next stage of the derivation, C excorporates and merges with the TP to form a projection of C, as demonstrated in (70) below.

(70)

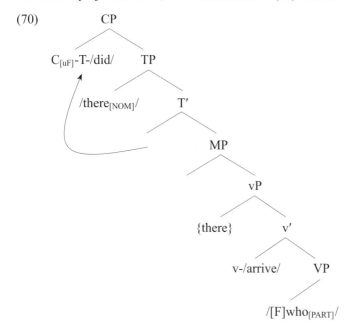

In (70), C with the uninterpretable focus feature [uF] serves as a probe and locates *who*, whose specifier position has the interpretable focus feature [F]. However, *who* cannot be raised to Spec-C, because as we observed in (66), it has become inactive with [PART], which means that the uninterpretable [uF] of the matrix C remains unchecked. Thus, (64a) is ungrammatical.[11]

Now let us turn to (64b). Suppose that the derivation proceeds to the stage where the VP is constructed by excorporation and merge of v-*arrive* with PredP, and raising of the associate *a driver of which car* from Spec-Pred to Spec-V.

(71)

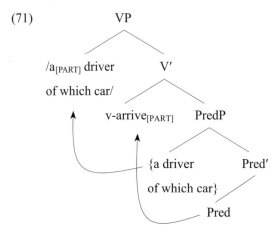

The partitive case [PART] is assigned to the D *a* by the unaccusative verb *arrive*, as demonstrated in (71) above.

In the next stage of the derivation, the unaccusative light verb v excorporates and merges with the VP to form a projection of v, to whose specifier *there* is merged, as shown in (72) below.

---

[11] Note that in (70), simultaneous identification of the *wh*-phrase *who* by the case-assigning head v and the phase head C does not hold: v and C do not constitute a lexical complex.

Chapter 5 Extraction from Subjects of Passive and Unaccusative Predicates   183

(72)

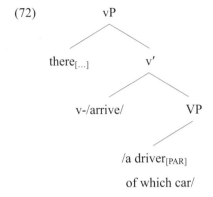

Let us now proceed to the stage where the TP is constructed by application of excorporation and merge of the lexical complex C-T-M (*did*). In (70), *there* is raised to Spec-T, where its unvalued case feature is valued as [NOM].

(73)

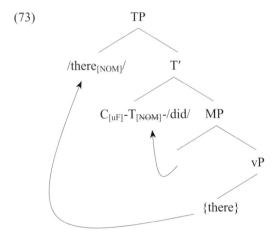

It should be remembered here that the associate DP in (64b) has a different structure than the one in (64a). In the case of (64b), an interpretable focus feature [F] is assigned to Spec-P, as demonstrated in (74).

(74) [DP a driver [PART] [PP [F]of which car]]

Now let us go back to the derivation. The C with an uninterpretable focus feature [uF] must excorporate and merge with the TP to form a projection of C, as shown in (75) below.

(75)

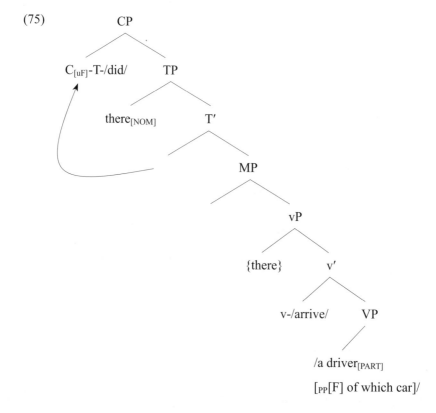

In (75), the C with the uninterpretable focus feature [uF] serves as a probe and locates a PP whose specifier has the interpretable focus feature [F]; thus, the PP *of which car* is attracted to Spec-C, as shown in (76) below. It goes without saying that the RIC does not preclude such subextraction of PP as observed in (76).

(76)

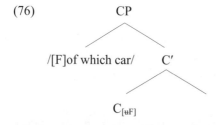

In (76), the uninterpretable focus feature [uF] of C is checked and deleted, and thus the derivation converges.

We have seen that our Excorporation Analysis, coupled with the derivation of the clause that contains *there* and an unaccusative verb, can explain the difference in grammatical acceptability between (64a) and (64b). However, there remains a problem with our analysis: in contrast with (64), repeated below as (78), no clear grammatical difference can be observed in a similar construction where the unaccusative verb *remain* appears.

(77) a. Of which drugs did there remain traces in the blood?
b. What did there remain in the blood?

(78) a. *Who did there arrive?
b. Of which car did there arrive a car?

It may be possible to attribute the grammatical difference between (77) and (78) to the meaning of the verbs. Although *remain* and *arrive* are both unaccusative verbs, they have different kinds of meanings: the former is a verb of existence and the other is a verb of manner of motion. I would like to leave this issue to future research.

5.4. Agreement in *there*-Constructions

We still have to clarify the agreement relation holding in *there*-constructions. We differ slightly from Chomsky (2001) in assuming that *there* has a case feature. For instance, the *there*'s in (79) are respectively assigned nominative case and accusative case by T and V (respectively).

(79) a. There arrived a driver of the car in the police station.
b. I believed there to arrive a driver of the car in the police station.

We also do not adopt Chomsky's assumption that structural case is a reflex of agreement. In other words, case-assignment and the agreement relation between case-assigner and associate are dissociated in our analysis. In order to comprehend this more clearly, let us examine (79) briefly. As observed above in this chapter, in 5.2 and 5.3, in a *there*-construction with the an accusative verb, an associate is generated in Spec-Pred and raised to Spec-V, where the associate is assigned partitive case by an unaccusative verb, as seen in (80) below.

(80) [$_{VP}$ /a driver$_{[PART]}$ of the car/ [$_{V'}$ v-arrive$_{[PART]}$ [$_{PredP}$ {a drive of the car} [$_{Pred'}$ Pred in the police station]]]]

The expletive is merged when the unaccusative light verb excorporates and merges with the VP, to form a vP.

(81) [vP there[...] [v' v-/arrive/ [VP a driver of the car [v' {arrive} [Pred {a driver of the car} [Pred' Pred in the police station]]]]]]

Suppose that the lexical complex C-T is merged to the structure in (81) and that *there* has the [3rd-person] feature, which is interpretable.[12]

(82) a. [TP C-T [vP there[...] [v' v-/arrive/ [VP a driver of the car
   b. T   there   a driver
      [α person], [α singular]   [3rd-person]   [3rd person] [+singular]

   c. T   there   a driver
      [3rd person], [+singular] [3rd-person]   [3rd person] [+singular]
   d. [TP /There[NOM]/ [T' C-T[NOM] [vP {there} [v' v-/arrive/ [VP a driver of the car

Here, agreement successfully holds between T and *there* as well as the associate *a driver of the car*, as represented in (82b) and as a result, the unvalued features of T are valued, as represented in (82c); *there* is also raised to Spec-T for case-theoretic reasons, as observed in (82d).

A similar derivation can be observed in the object-raising construction. Suppose that the lexical complex v*-*believe-to* is merged with the embedded vP, and that the matrix VP is constructed by excorporation and merge of the lexical complex, as seen in (83).

(83) a. [VP v*-believed [MP to [vP there[...] [v' v-/arrive/ [VP a driver of the car
   b. believed   there   a driver
      [α person] [α singular] [3rd person]   [3rd person] [+singular]

   c. believed   there   a driver
      [3rd person] [+singular] [3rd person]   [3rd person] [+singular]
   d. [vP there[ACC] [VP v*-believed [MP to [vP {there} [v' v-/arrive/ [VP a driver

---

[12] Following Radford (2009), we assume that *there* has [3rd person] feature.

Agreement successfully multiply holds here between *proved* and *there*/the associate *a driver of the car*, as represented in (83b); as a result, unvalued features of the verb *proved* are valued, as represented in (83c). In (83d), *there* is raised to Spec-V for case-theoretic reasons.

It can be concluded from the observation in (82) and (83) that case-assignment and φ-feature agreement can be dissociated in the *there*-construction.

5.5. Summary

In this chapter, we have analyzed extraction from subjects of passives and unaccusative predicates. We have shown that subextraction from subjects (or associates, in the case of unaccusative *there*-constructions) can be accounted for in terms of the Excorporation Analysis. We have also proposed a functional category α for passives whose role is absorption of accusative case of passive verbs and determination of the morphological form of the verbs. In addition to these functions, it optionally assigns partitive case to the passive verbs, which makes it possible to derive *there*-constructions in passive sentences.

Chapter 6

Summary and Conclusion

Much of the discussion in this book centers on the analysis of subextraction from, and total extraction of, subjects. It has been widely recognized that subextraction of a *wh*-phrase out of a subject gives rise to ungrammaticality, which led Huang (1982), working within the framework of Government and Binding Theory, to propose the Subject Condition. Since then, many attempts have been made to give a principled explanation to this phenomenon. Among such attempts lies Chomsky's (1986) analysis according to which ungrammaticality of the Subject Condition can be reduced to violation of the Subjacency Condition and the Empty Category Principle (ECP). Much of the descriptive and theoretical apparatus proposed under the framework of Government and Binding Theory lost their status in the early 1990s when Chomsky proposed the Minimalist Program, because this program requires that the apparatus be minimized, including discarding constructs such as the Subjacency Condition and ECP. Many proposals have been made to account for the Subject Condition in the framework of the Minimalist Program. The most promising approach seems to me to be the one proposed in Chomsky (2008), in which he attributes ungrammaticality of the Subject Condition to violation of the Locality Condition and the Inactivity Condition, based on his Phase Theory. The data he analyzes in that study are the kind of data traditionally or conventionally considered in relation to this issue, where subextraction takes place from the subject position of simple clauses.

(1) *Of which car did the driver cause the accident?

However, scrutinizing other, more unusual data reveals that there are grammatical constructions that tolerate subextraction of a *wh*-phrase from a subject. For instance, this phenomenon can be found in subextraction from an infinitival subject introduced with a prepositional complementizer *for*.

(2) Of which major is it important for students to take a course in physics?

Under Chomsky's phase-based account, it would be impossible for a *wh*-phrase to be extracted from an infinitival subject, because subextraction from Spec-v* and from Spec-T violate his Locality Condition and Inactivity Condition, respectively.

Given this state of affairs, we introduced in Chapter 2 the Excorporation Analysis by Tonoike (2008) as a structure-building tool, according to which an English sentence is built by excorporation and subsequent merge of a lexical complex v*-V and C-T. Applying the Excorporation Analysis to the infinitival clause, we assume that the embedded CP phase is constructed by excorporation of a lexical head C-T(*for*)-M(*to*). Adopting the Overt Syntax Hypothesis of Tonoike (2008), we assume that movement of an element must always carry a phonetic form, leaving behind the meaning as a copy in the base-generated position. This assumption makes it possible to reduce Chomsky's Locality Condition to violation of the Overt Syntax Hypothesis: when a subject containing a *wh*-phrase moves from Spec-v*, the syntactic operation cannot move the *wh*-phrase from Spec-v* because it does not have a phonetic form. It then follows that subextraction from a subject should be executed from Spec-T. This has led us to propose the Revised Inactivity Condition (RIC), which states that the D and N of a DP, which are case-assigned, become inactive, but other elements are not. Due to this condition, the *wh*-PP can be extracted from the DP in Spec-T.

(3) [$_{CP}$ /of which major/ [$_{C'}$ for [$_{TP}$ $_{DP}$ /the$_{[ACC]}$ students {of which major}/ to take a course in physics]]]?

We have also seen that this account can explain the grammatical sentence where a *wh*-phrase is extracted from the subject of a finite embedded clause.

(4) Of which car is it likely that the driver will cause a scandal?

The *wh*-phrase in (4) can also successfully be extracted from the subject of the finite embedded clause, in the same manner as subextraction from the subject of an infinitival clause.

(5) [$_{CP}$ /of which car/ [$_{C'}$ that [$_{TP}$ $_{DP}$/the$_{[NOM]}$ driver {of which car}/ will cause a scandal]]]?

We then examined how our Excorporation Analysis can exclude a typical example of Subject Condition violation.

(6) *Of which car did the drive cause a scandal?

Adopting Tonoike's (2000) analysis concerning *wh*-movement, we demonstrated that the sentence in (6) can be excluded by the assumption that *wh*-movement is triggered by focus feature checking. An uninterpretable focus feature [uF] is assigned to the phase head, and an interpretable focus feature [F] is assigned to any Spec of the category that is to be moved. In (7), an interpretable focus feature [F] is assigned to Spec-P in the subject phrase, which makes it impossible to check an uninterpretable focus feature [uF] of v* when the subject is merged to Spec-v* for θ-theoretic reasons.

(7) *[$_{v*P}$ [$_{DP}$ the driver [$_{PP}$ [F] of which car]] v*$_{[uF]}$ cause a scandal]

A grammatical counterpart to (6) can be derived if an interpretable focus feature [F] is assigned to the topmost Spec-D.

(8) a. The driver of which car caused a scandal?
   b. [$_{v*}$ [$_{DP}$ [F] the driver of which car] v*$_{[uF]}$ -cause a scandal]]

In Chapter 3, we applied our Excorporation Analysis to total extraction of the *wh*-phrase from a subject of an embedded clauses—the Overt Complementizer Copy (Trace) effect. We first observed how Chomsky's (1986) Minimality and Rizzi's (1990) Relativized Minimality analyzed this effect and examined difficulties these two analyses faced. As an alternative, we proposed to apply our Excorporation Analysis, coupled with the RIC, to overt complementizer copy effect. Among overt complementizer copy effects, we begin with *for*-copy effects.

(9) a. *Who is it important for who to take a course in physics?
   b. *[$_{CP}$ C-for [$_{TP}$ /who$_{[ACC]}$/ [$_{T'}$ {for} [$_{MP}$ to [$_{v*P}$ {who}

(9) can be excluded in terms of violation of the RIC: when the infinitival subject *who* is moved to Spec-T, it becomes inactive, because *who* is the D assigned accusative case by *for* and is also the head of an A-chain.

We further extend our Excorporation Analysis to the explanation of the *that*-copy effect and its grammatical counterpart.

(10) a. *Who do you think that will see Mary?
 b. Who do you think will see Mary?

We posit different derivation and structure for an embedded finite clause, depending on whether it has an overt C (*that*) or a covert C. When an embedded clause has an overt C, it does not constitute a lexical complex with T, and thus the overt C merges with the TP after the subject moves to Spec-T, for case-theoretic reasons.

(11) a. [$_{TP}$ /who$_{[NOM]}$/ [$_{T'}$ T-/will/ [$_{MP}$ {will} [$_{v*P}$ {who}
 b. *[$_{CP}$ /who$_{[NOM]}$/ [$_{C'}$ that [$_{TP}$ {who} [$_{T'}$ T-/will/ [$_{MP}$ {will} [$_{v*P}$ {who}

The ungrammaticality of (10a) can be reduced to violation of the RIC: the subject *who* becomes inactive in (11a), and thus it is impossible to extract it as in (11b). In the case of (10b), the null complementizer constitutes a lexical complex with T (and Mod(al)), and the embedded clause is constructed by excorporation and subsequent merge. The derived embedded clause is CP as well as TP. This dual status of the embedded clause makes it possible for *who* whose unvalued case feature is valued as [NOM] to move further away in the sentence.

(12) [$_{v*P}$ v*$_{[uF]}$-think [$_{VP}$ {think} [$_{CP/TP}$ [F]/who$_{[NOM]}$/ [$_{C'/T'}$ C$_{[uF]}$-T-/will/ [$_{MP}$ {will} [$_{v*P}$ {who} ...]]]]]]

Seen from the matrix v*, case-assigned *who* occupies A-bar position, not A-position, which means that extraction is implemented without violating the RIC, since the latter is sensitive to the head of an A-chain, not an A-bar chain. Hence, (10b) is grammatical.

We have also examined subextraction from, and total extraction of, the subject of an infinitival complement of *want*.

(13) a. Of which car do you want the driver to avoid an accident?
 b. Of which car do you want very much for a driver to avoid an accident?

(14) a. Who do you want to avoid an accident?
 b. *Who do you want very much for to avoid an accident?

The (un)grammaticality of these sentences can be accounted for in the manner that we have proposed in this book.

Our analysis was also evaluated by comparison with the analysis by

Rizzi and Shlonsky (2007). Their analysis heavily depends on Criterial Freezing to exclude overt complementizer trace effects. To do so, a seemingly new functional projection SubjP must be posited above the TP: when a *wh*-subject is situated in Spec-Subj, it is frozen in place. We have pointed out that contrary to this approach, there is no conceptual necessity for postulating SubjP; this problem is similar to that of AgrP, which was posited in the early Minimalist era, and abolished in Chomsky (1995). Keeping to Criterial Freezing and postulated SubjP bring out another difficulty: obviating overt complementizer trace effects; this is implemented by Skipping Strategy, which calls for additional unnatural mechanisms. We have concluded that if we keep to the Strong Minimalist Thesis, SubjP should be dispensed with.

In Chapter 4, we investigated extraction from objects of transitive verbs and objects of prepositions. The phenomena cast doubt on our Excorporation Analysis, because extraction from objects always takes place from case-assigned positions: the objects are case-assigned when first merged with a transitive verb or preposition.

(15) a. Who do you see?
 b. Which city do you live in?

In order to solve this problem, Egashira and Tonoike (2010, 2012) proposed that simultaneous syntactic operations can provide a loophole to avoid violation of the RIC. These operations are (i) case valuation holding between V/P and its *wh*-object and (ii) *wh*-identification holding between a phase head and a *wh*-object. These simultaneous syntactic operations are observed only in extraction from objects of V and P, not from Subjects. We made an attempt to reduce this reliance on simultaneous syntactic operations to a more natural condition. This condition can be observed in subject extraction from a *that*-less embedded clause: when a *wh*-subject occupies sentence-initial position in the embedded clause, it occupies Spec-C and Spec-T at the same time. Seen from the perspective of the embedded clause, it occupies Spec-T, that is, A-position; and seen from a matrix clause, it occupies Spec-C, or A-bar position. The same is true of the objects of V and P. Seen from the perspective of a case-assigner V and P, the object occupies A-position. In other words, the *wh*-phrase is a head of trivial A-chain. Seen from a phase head, the *wh*-phrase occupies A-bar position; in other words, it is a head of a trivial A-bar chain. When the *wh*-phrase is attracted from the matrix v*, it can be assumed to be attracted from an A-bar position.

Chapter 5 analyzed extraction from subjects of passive predicates and from subjects and associates of unaccusative predicates. We began with extraction from subjects of passive predicates, based on the analysis of the derivation of passives by Egashira and Tonoike (2012), and we have observed that *wh*-extraction from a subject is implemented from base-generated position.

As for the unaccusative verbs, we have proposed that they are of two types: one with no case features at all, and the other with partitive case feature. The latter type accommodates the expletive *there*, which we assume is generated in the specifier position of the unaccusative light verb, in accordance with Deal (2009).

We also analyzed *wh*-extraction from associates of *there*-constructions whose verbs take a passive form. We proposed that the passive α has a function of assigning partitive case feature to the verb, and that *there* is base-generated in Spec-α. This derivation makes it possible to extract a *wh*-phrase from the construction.

Thus, in this book, we have observed that the Excorporation Analysis together with the RIC can account for subextraction from, and total extraction of, subjects of various types of predicates. It can be concluded on this basis that extraction from a subject can occur as freely as that from an object, as long as the RIC is observed. In other words, there is no Subject Condition in the sense of Huang (1982) and extraction can be applied freely in Overt Syntax.

References

Bach, Emmon (1977) "Review of Paul M. Postal *On Raising*," *Language* 53, 621-654.

Baltin, Mark (1995) "Floating Quantifiers, PRO and Predication," *Linguistic Inquiry* 26, 199-248.

Baltin, Mark (2006) "Extraposition," *The Blackwell Companion to Syntax, volume II*, ed. by Martin Everaert and Henk van Riemsdijk, 237-271, Basil Blackwell, Oxford.

Belletti, Adriana (1988) "The Case of Unaccusatives," *Linguistic Inquiry* 19, 1-34.

Belletti, Adriana (1990) *Generalized Verb Movement*, Rosenberg & Sellier, Turin.

Bošković, Željko (1995) *Principles of Economy in Nonfinite Complementation*, Doctoral dissertation, University of Connecticut.

Bošković, Željko (1996) "Selection and Categorial Status of Infinitival Complements," *Natural Language and Linguistic Theory* 14, 269-304.

Bošković, Željko (1997) *The Syntax of Nonfinite Complementation: An Economy Approach*, MIT Press, Cambridge, MA.

Bošković, Željko (2007) "Agree, Phases, and Intervention Effects," *Linguistic Analysis* 33, 54-96.

Bowers, John (2002) "Transitivity," *Linguistic Inquiry* 33, 183-224.

Bruzio, Luigi (1986) *Italian Syntax*, Kluwer, Dordrecht.

Chomsky, Noam (1973) "Conditions on Transformation," *A Festschrift for Morris Halle*, ed. by Stephen Anderson and Paul Kiparsky, 232-286, Holt, Rinehart, and Winston, New York.

Chomsky, Noam (1981) *Lectures on Government and Binding Theory*, Foris, Dordrecht.

Chomsky, Noam (1986a) *Barriers*, MIT Press, Cambridge, MA.

Chomsky, Noam (1986b) *Knowledge of Language: Its Nature, Origin and Use*, Praeger, New York.

Chomsky, Noam (1993) "A Minimalist Program for Linguistic Theory," *The View from Building 20*, ed. by Kenneth Hale and Samuel Jay Keyser, 1–52, MIT Press, Cambridge, MA.

Chomsky, Noam (1994) "Bare Phrase Structure," MIT Occasional Papers in Lunguistics 5. Department of Linguistics and Philosophy, MIT.

Chomsky, Noam (1995) *The Minimalist Program*, MIT Press, Cambridge, MA.

Chomsky, Noam (2000) "Minimalist Inquiries," *Step by Step: Essays in Minimalist Syntax in Honor of Howard Lasnik*, ed. by Roger Martin, David Michaels and Juan Uriagereka, 9–155, MIT Press, Cambridge, MA.

Chomsky, Noam (2001) "Derivation by Phase," *Ken Hale: A Life in Language*, ed. by Michael Kenstowicz, MIT Press, Cambridge, MA.

Chomsky, Noam (2004) "Beyond Explanatory Adequacy," *Structures and Beyond—The Cartography of Syntactic Structures, vol. 3*, ed. by Adrena Belletti, 104–131, Oxford University Press, Oxford.

Chomsky, Noam (2006) "Approaching UG from Below," *Interfaces + Recursion = Language? Chomsky's Minimalism and the View from Semantics*, ed. by Uli Sauerland and Hans-Martin Gartner, Mouton de Gruyter, Berlin.

Chomsky, Noam (2008) "On Phases," *Foundational Issues in Linguistic Theory: Essays in Honor of Jean Roger Vergnaud*, ed. by Robert Fredin, Carlos P. Otero and Maria Luisa Zubizarreta, 133–166, MIT Press, Cambridge, MA.

Chomsky, Noam (2013) "Problems of Projection," *Lingua* 130, 33–49.

Chomsky, Noam (2014) "Syntax Session," Keio Linguistic Colloqium, March 8, 2014, Keio University.

Chomsky, Noam and Howard Lasnik (1977) "Filters and Control," *Linguistic Inquiry* 8, 425–504.

Chomsky, Noam and Howard Lasnik (1995) "The Theory of Principles and Parameters," *The Minimalist Program*, ed. by Noam Chomsky, 13–127, MIT Press, Cambridge, MA.

Citko, Barbara (2014) *Phase Theory: An Introduction*, Cambridge University Press, Cambridge.

Deal, A. Rose (2009) "The Origin and Content of Expletives: Evidence from Selection," *Syntax* 12:4, 285–323.

Egashira, Hiroki and Shigeo Tonoike (2010) "The Inactivity Condition and An Excorporation Analysis of Head-Movement," presentation given at the 141th Annual Conference of the Linguistic Society of Japan, November 27, 2010.

Egashira, Hiroki and Shigeo Tonoike (2012) "The Inactivity Condition and an Excorporation Analysis of Head-Movement," ms.

Emonds, Joseph (1985) *A Unified Theory of Syntactic Categories*, Foris, Dordrecht.

Grimshaw, Jane (1993) "Minimal Projections, Heads, and Optimality," ms., Rutgers University.

Groat, Erich (1995) "English Expletives: A Minimalist Approach," *Linguistic Inquiry* 26, 354–365.

Haegeman, Liliane (1991) *Introduction to Government and Binding Theory*, Black-

well, Oxford.
Haegeman, Liliane, Angel Jiménez-Fernández and Andrew Radford (2014) "Deconstructing the Subject Condition in Terms of Cumulative Constraint Violation," *Linguistic Review* 31:1, 73–150.
Haider, Hubert (2010) *The Syntax of German*, Cambridge University Press, Cambridge.
Hay, Jennifer, Christopher Kennedy and Beth Levin (1999) "Scalar Structure Underlies Telicity in 'Degree Achievements'," *Proceedings of SALT 9*, 127–144, Cornell Linguistics Circle Publications, Ithaca, NY.
Hiraiwa, Ken (2005) *Dimensions of Symmetry in Syntax: Agreement and Clausal Architecture*, Doctoral dissertation, MIT.
Huang, C.-T. James (1982) *Logical Relations in Chinese and the Theory of Grammar*, Doctoral Dissertation, MIT.
Jackendoff, Ray (1972) *Semantic Interpretation in Generative Grammar*, MIT Press, Cambridge, MA.
Jackendoff, Ray (1992) *Language of the Mind: Essays on Mental Representation*, MIT Press, Cambridge, MA.
Jackendoff, Ray (1996) *The Architecture of the Language Faculty*, MIT Press, Cambridge, MA.
Jaeggli, A. Osvaldo (1986) "Passive," *Linguistic Inquiry* 17, 587–622.
Johnson, Kyle (1985) *A Case for Movement*, Doctoral dissertation, MIT.
Kobayashi, Keiichiro (2009) "Effects of Pied-Piping on Extraction from Subject in English," *Kagaku/Ningen* 40, 31–57.
Kuno, Susumu (1973) "Constraints on Internal Clauses and Sentential Subjects," *Linguistic Inquiry* 3, 363–385.
Kuroda, Shige-Yuki (1988) "Whether We Agree or Not: A Comparative Syntax of English and Japanese," *Lingvisticae Investigationes* 12, 1–47.
Laka, Itziar (1990) *Negation in Syntax: On the Nature of Functional Categories and Projetions*, Doctoral dissertation, Massachusetts Institute of Technology.
Lakoff, George (1968) "Pronouns and Reference," ms., Indiana University, Bloomington.
Lasnik, Howard (1992) "Case and Expletives: Notes toward a Parametric Account," *Linguistic Inquiry* 23, 381–405.
Lasnik, Howard (1995) "Case and Expletives Revisited: On Greed and Other Human Failings," *Linguistic Inquiry* 26, 615–633.
Lasnik, Howard (2001) "Subjects, Objects and the EPP," *Objects and Other Subjects*, ed. by William D. Davies and Stanley Dubinsky, 103–121. Kluwer, Dordrecht.
Lasnik, Howard and Mamoru Saito (1991) "On the Subject of Infinitives," *CLS* 27, ed. by L. M. Dobrin, L. Nichols and R. M. Rodriguez.
Lasnik, Howard and Mamoru Saito (1992) *Move α: Conditions on Its Applications and Outputs*, MIT Press, Cambridge, MA.
Legate, J. Anne (2003) "Some Interface Properties of the Phase," *Linguistic Inquiry* 39, 55–101.
Legate, J. Anne (2014) *Voice and viLessons from Acehnese* MIT, Cambridge, MA.

Levin, Beth and Malka Rappaport Hovav (1995) *Unaccusativity at the Syntax-Lexical Semantic Interface*, MIT Press, Cambridge, MA.

Levin, Beth and Malka Rappaport Hovav (1999) "Change of State Verbs: Implications for Theories of Argument Projection," *BLS* 28, 269–280.

Lumsden, Michael (1988) *Existential Sentences: Their Structure and Meaning*, Croom Helm, London.

Martin, Roger (2001) "Null Case and the Distribution of PRO," *Linguistic Inquiry* 32, 141–166.

Matsubara, Fuminori (2002) "A Minimalist Approach to *to*-Infinitival Complements in Belfast English," *English Linguistics* 19:2, 239–265.

Matsubara, Fuminori (2008) "Remarks on Chomsky's (2008) Analysis of Extraction from Subject," *English Linguistics* 25:2, 464–474.

May, Robert (1977) *The Grammar of Quantification*, Doctoral dissertation, MIT.

May, Robert (1985) *Logical Form*, MIT Press, Cambridge, MA.

Milsark, Gary (1974) *Existential Sentences in English*, Indiana University Linguistics Club, Bloomington.

Nakajima, Heizo (1991) "Reduced Clauses and Argumenthood of AgrP," *Topics in Small Clauses*, ed. by Heizo Nakajima and Shigeo Tonoike, 39–57, Kurosio, Tokyo.

Nomura, Tadao (2006) *ModalP and Subjunctive Present*, Hituzi Syobo, Tokyo.

Pesetsky, David (1982) *Paths and Categories*, Doctoral dissertation, MIT.

Pesetsky, David and Esther Torrego (2001) "T-to-C Movement: Causes and Consequences," *Ken Hale: A Life in Language*, ed. by Michael Kenstowicz, 355–426, MIT Press, Cambridge, MA.

Pollock, Jean-Yves (1989) "Verb Movement, Universal Grammar, and the Structure of IP," *Linguistic Inquiry* 20, 365–424.

Postal, Paul (1966) "On So-Called 'Pronouns; in English," *Report of the Seventeenth Annual Round Table Meeting on Linguistics and Language Studies*, ed. by Francis P. Dinneen, 177–206, Georgetown University Press, Washington, D.C.

Postal, Paul (1974) *On Raising*, MIT Press, Cambridge, MA.

Radford, Andrew (2009) *Analysing English Sentences: A Minimalist Approach*, Cambridge University Press, Cambridge.

Rizzi, Luigi (1990) *Relativized Minimality*, MIT Press, Cambridge, MA.

Rizzi, Luigi (2004) "On the Cartography of Syntactic Structures," *The Structure of CP and IP*, ed. by Luigi Rizzi, 3–15, Oxford University Press, New York.

Rizzi, Luigi (2006) "On the Form of Chains: Criterial Positions and ECP Effects," *On Wh-Movement*, ed. by Lisa Cheng and Norbert Corber, 97–133, MIT Press, Cambridge, MA.

Rizzi, Luigi (2007) "On Some Properties of Criterial Freezing," *Studies in Linguistics* 1, 145–158.

Rizzi, Luigi (2012) "*Cartography, Criteria, and Labeling*," ms.

Rizzi, Luigi and Ur Shlonsky (2007) "Strategies of Subject Extraction," *Interfaces + Recursion = Language?*, ed. by Hans-Martin Gärtner and Uli Sauerland, 115–160, Mouton de Gruyter, Berlin.

Roberts, Ian (1991) "Excorporation and Minimality," *Linguistic Inquiry* 22, 209–218.
Ross, John (1967) *Constraints on Variables in Syntax*, Doctoral dissertation, MIT.
Safir, Ken (1985) *Syntactic Chains and the Definiteness Effect*, Doctoral dissertation, MIT.
Stowell, Tim (1982) "The Tense of Infinitives," *Linguistic Inquiry* 13, 561–570.
Svenonius, Peter (2004) "On the Edge," *Peripheries: Syntactic Edges and their Effects*, ed. by David Adger, Cecile de Cat and George Tsoulas, 259–287, Springer, Dordrecht.
Taraldsen, K. Tarald (1978) "On the NIC, Vacuous Application and the *That*-trace Filter," ms., MIT.
Taraldsen, K. Tarald (2001) "Subject Extraction, the Distribution of Expletives and Stylistic Inversion," *Subject Inversion in Romance and the Theory of Universal Grammar*, ed. by Aafke Hulk and Jean-Yves Pollock, 163–182, Oxford University Press, New York.
Tonoike, Shigeo (1999) "Agreement as Dislocated Morphological Features," *Metropolitan Linguistics* 19, 1–21.
Tonoike, Shigeo (2000) "Wh-Movement, Pied-Piping and Related Matters," *Grant-in-Aid for COE Research Report (4): Researching and Verifying an Advanced Theory of Human Language: Explanation of the Human Faculty for Constructing and Computing Sentences on the Basis of Lexical Conceptual Features*, 210–227.
Tonoike, Shigeo (2008a) "The General Minimalist Framework," ms., University of Hawaii and Aoyama Gakuin University.
Tonoike, Shigeo (2008b) "Minimalisuto Puroguramu (Minimalist Program)," *Gengogaku-no Ryooiki (i)* (The Domain of Linguistics (i)), ed. by Heizo Nakajima, 135–168, Asakura Publishing, Tokyo.

Index

A
absorption   156, 162, 176
Accusative -ing gerunds   140–150
Agree(ment)   8–9
arrive   179–185

B
Bare Phrase Structure   11–12
barrier   3–4, 16, 73–74
Belletti, A.   112, 169
Bošković, Z.   25, 35, 96
Bowers, J.   165

C
Case Adjacency Condition   46
case-assignment under Merge   35, 43, 123, 177
causative construction   140
Chomsky, N.   2–6, 8–13, 16, 18–20, 21–26, 32–37, 40, 46, 57, 72–74, 78–81, 113, 121, 123, 138, 179, 185, 189–191, 193
Citko, B.   5, 8
Clause Non-Final Incomplete Constituent Constraint   40
Condition on Extraction Domain (CED)   3
Conceptual-intentioal (CI) system   5–6
copy   11–12, 30, 36, 50
Criterial Freezing   104–105

D
Defective Intervention Effect   46
Deal, A. Rose   47, 170–171, 176, 194
derivation   12–20
dual syntactic category   93

E
economy   56
 derivational economy   66, 68, 95, 160
Edge Feature (EF)   18, 21, 49, 151
Egashira, H. and S. Tonoike   124, 126, 156, 162, 193–194
Emonds, J.   46, 56
Empty Category Principle (ECP)   3, 72, 103, 120, 189
extraction
 total Extraction   1, 71–115

201

subextraction 1, 57
EPP (Extended Projection Principle) 24, 35, 106
Excorporation Analysis 32, 41, 81
Exceptional Case Marking 15-18, 96, 132-140
expletive 53, 107, 112
expletive *there* 165, 170-172, 176-178
Extension Condition 33-34, 36

F
features 6-8
for (infinitival complementizer as T) 42, 83
focus feature 59
Focus Movement 59

G
Goal 8
government 4, 16, 46
 head-government 74-75, 80
 θ government 74
Government and Binding (GB) Theory 3, 73, 189

H
head-movement 33
Huang, C.-T. J. 3, 57, 189, 194

I
Inactivity Condition 4, 19, 23, 40

K
Kuno, S. 40
Kobayashi, K. 32, 54

L
Lasnik, H and M. Saito 15-16, 96, 141
lexical array (LA) 5-6
Levin, B and H. Rappaport 169

light adjective α 156
Locality Condition (LC) 4, 22, 151, 189

M
Matsubara, F. 31, 46, 150-151
Merge
 Internal Merge (IM) 9, 10, 47
 External Merge (EM) 9, 10, 47
Minimality
 Rigid Minimality 72-73
 Relativized Minimality 74-78
Modal Phrase (MP) 43, 83

N
Nakajima, H. 140
Nomura, T. 43
Numeration 5, 11

O
operator for yes-no interrogatives 39
Object Raising Construction 132-140, 140-155
Overt Syntax Hypothesis 36, 45, 50, 64
Overt C trace (copy) effect
 that-trace effect 71, 74, 90
 that-copy effect 86, 90, 110
 for-trace effect 71, 81
 for-copy effect 82, 91

P
partitive case [PART] 169, 174, 176, 180, 182
passive predicates 155
perceptual construction 150
phase 12-20
phase head 12
Pollock, J.-Y. 112
Postal, M. 15, 133
Predication Phrase (PredP) 165-166
Probe 8

R
Radford, A.   29, 155, 165
Revised Inactivity Condition   50, 85, 94, 120
Rizzi, L.   74–78, 80–81, 86, 104, 106–107, 109–110, 113, 191
Rizzi, L and Shlonsky, U.   103–107, 109–115, 193
Ross, J.   59

S
sensorimotor system   5–6
simultaneous syntactic relation   124–132
Skipping Strategies   107, 110–112
subject-object asymmetry   1, 2, 103–105
Subject Condition   1, 3, 21, 29, 31, 32, 41, 47, 57
Subject Criterion   103, 106–107, 109–113
Subject Island   2
Subject Phrase (SubjP)   106–113

Subjacency Condition   3, 4, 189
Strong Minimalist Thesis (SMT)   5, 9, 10, 193

T
θ-feature   62–63, 161
Transfer   12
to (infinitival)   43
Tonoike, S.   32–36, 41, 59, 62–63, 92, 119–120, 124, 126, 156, 158, 162, 169, 190–191, 193–194

U
unaccusative predicates   155–187
unaccusative light verb v   166, 170, 180, 182

W
want   95–103

On Extraction from Subjects: An Excorporation Account

著 者　江頭浩樹

発行者　武村哲司

2016年12月17日　第1版第1刷発行©

発行所　株式会社　開 拓 社
　　　　〒113-0023　東京都文京区向丘1-5-2
　　　　電話　(03)5842-8900（代表）
　　　　振替　00160-8-39587
　　　　http://www.kaitakusha.co.jp

印刷　株式会社　あるむ　　　　ISBN978-4-7589-2235-7　C3080